Twila's Dilemma

Field of Lies; Touchdown in Truth

The Harriet High Series

Printed in the United States of America

Cover Design: Independent Designer

Formatting & Consulting:
LPW Editing & Consulting Services, LLC
The Editorial Midwife Publishing
www.litapward.com

First Printing, 2019
ISBN – 978-1-7343853-0-4

Books by Yolanda

For Teens:

Harriet High Series

Mysteries of Harriet High: "The Secret of Twila Anderson"

Mommy's Girl

Summer Rain

For Adults:

Wolf in Sheep's Clothing

Eyes of the Enemy

Twila's Dilemma

Field of Lies; Touchdown in Truth

Yolanda Randolph

The Harriet High Series

PROLOGUE

Stop! Hey! Adriana, Stop! You're going to get us kill—"

"Shut up Twila! Just sit back and chill! I got you!"

Twila held onto the passenger seat in her best friend's car. Catching quick glimpses out of the window, she saw nothing but hard rain falling and blustery trees whipping by extremely fast in the dusk filled sky. The sidewalks were unusually bare, and the streets were just as empty. "Ugh!" Twila yelled as Adriana rounded a sharp corner without slowing down.

"Adriana!"

"Twila! Calm down girl! Just chill and enjoy the ride."

Twila's mind was full of fear and anger, a feeling that she's never felt before. *I am going to punch her dead in the mouth when I get out of here; if I'm alive.* Closing her eyes, she thought of her mother and her father; thinking of all the trouble she was going to be in once they found out that she decided to get in the car with Adriana, knowing that she had been drinking. *Why did I get in this car? Why did I...* "Woah!" She screamed as Adriana rolled over a row of jagged train tracks, not bothering at all to look out for her tires. Closing her eyes tighter, Twila thought of her grandmother and the words she would speak if she was in a bad situation. *God can help you through all things. Always trust in Him,* she heard her grandmother's voice. Closing her eyes even tighter, to the point where she thought they would burst, she began to call out in prayer. *God, please help me,* she chanted quietly while holding on for dear life to the side of her seat. She looked over at Adriana and was in shock at the sight of a big grin plastered on her face. "This chick is crazy!" She yelled, not caring what Adriana thought of her statement. In an instant, Adriana slammed on her brakes. The car slid onto the sidewalk and jolted out of its movement. A thick cloud of smoke replaced the rain that had fallen minutes prior and entered high into the sky, causing a crowd to rapidly form. Twila opened her eyes and immediately felt all over her body. "Thank God!" She called out as everything felt like it was in place.

"Hey! Are you alright?!" A man yelled from the crowd.

"Somebody call the police and the ambulance!" Another man shouted.

Feeling a trickle fall down the side of her head, Twila gasped and rubbed the spot, noticing a gash there. "Aw man," she sighed. "Adr... Adriana!" Suddenly, she remembered that Adriana was the one driving; the one who caused the crash. "Oh no! Adriana!" She looked over at her friend and screamed out in horror at the sight of her limp body.

"Adriana!"

"Oh God! Somebody please help me!"

Pulling on the door handle, she yelled out in agony at the pain that was ripping through her hand. This door is stuck! "Somebody help me!"

"Hold on! We tryin' to get it open!"

Twila watched in full panic mode while two men worked their hardest to pry the door open.

"Oh Lord! The car is smoking!" A woman yelled from the crowd.

"Oh God!" Twila seethed, feeling as if she was going to pass out at any moment. Glancing back over at Adriana, a fresh flow of tears began to fall fast down her face.

"Adriana! Get up!"

"No...no...no... I got to get out of here." Twila looked out at the frantic faces that stared back at her. Panic and fear gripped her like a glove that was entirely too small.

"This car is getting ready to blow up! We got to get them out of there!"

"I think the girl in the driver side is dead!"

"Oh my God! No!"

"Oh shoot! It's on fire!"

"No!" Twila yelled as she fumbled with the door as hard as she could to get out the car.

CHAPTER 1

"Adriana, I promise it's going to be okay," Twila said to her best friend, as she flopped down on her oversized beanbag and put her feet up on her desk. "Just go in and blend in with everybody else. Nobody is thinking about what happened all those many months ago. They are on to the next thing."

"Yeah, that's easy for you to say," Adriana huffed. "You weren't the one sent away for murdering the star of the football team. Harriet's High's number one at that."

Twila lowered the volume on her phone and looked towards her bedroom door. She smiled at her small Yorkie, Maddie, as she entered the bedroom and laid down beside her.

"Adriana, you didn't *murder* Kyle so stop saying that. It was an accident, and everybody understands that. You had a problem; made the mistake of trying alcohol and you learned from it. What did the doctors teach you at Holly Grove?"

Twila frowned as she watched Adriana put her head down. Adriana remained silent and stared off into space. The mention of Holly Grove always changed Adriana's demeanor but never to this extent.

"Adriana?"

"Yeah, I'm good," Adriana replied. "Holly Grove is in my past. You know I hated that place and don't like talking about it."

"Yeah," Twila said softly.

"So, what's good with you and Josh? We've been on the phone for almost an hour and I haven't heard you mention him."

"Josh," Twila muttered as she closed her eyes and thought of her boyfriend. They got together soon after Adriana went away and right after the harsh reality that Kyle was gone forever. The memories began to sink into Twila's mind. Not only did Twila have a rough time with her new reality of Kyle's fate but Josh did too. Mourning the loss of his best friend and Twila mourning the loss of her crush, they mourned together and soon their mourning blossomed into a relationship.

"Uh, chick?"

Twila opened her eyes and chuckled. *Okay, Twila thought quietly. Let's just change the subject then.* "I don't know. It's like he's different or something. I don't know how to explain it. One minute he's cool and the next, he's yelling at me. I think he blames me for Kyle's dea... the accident," she glanced at Adriana, quickly changing her words. "Since I was in the car that night, I guess."

"Well, don't worry about him. There's plenty of boys who would love to be in his spot."

"Yeah, I guess so," Twila replied while gently petting her puppy. Anxious to get the conversation off Josh and his funny acting attitude, Twila smiled at Adriana. "So, what's good with your parents?"

Adriana chuckled. "They good, I guess. I think my mother is tired of fussing at my dad and finally getting used to the idea that I'm living with him now."

"Yeah, I hope so," Twila said sympathetically.

Squeals and screams from the neighborhood kids echoed through Twila's room from the open window.

"I got it!" One of the kids screamed.

"Dang," Twila mumbled as Maddie hopped up and began to growl.

"Too late!" Another kid called.

"And the barking begins," Twila said as Maddie ran full speed out of Twila's room, down the stairs, and towards the back door; barking loudly the entire time.

"Can't you get Maddie trained or something," Adriana laughed.

"Hush up Maddie!" Twila heard her mother yell.

"Twila! Come and get Maddie!"

Twila shook her head and prepared to get up from the comforts of her beanbag.

"Coming Ma!" She called out.

"Ugh, I wish I could, but I don't have the money for all that. I'm supposed to start babysitting a little girl from my grandma's church, but her father hasn't called me yet."

"Oh," Adriana responded. "You should stop with the babysitting and get a job at Crust. I heard they were hiring."

"Yep, already applied," Twila replied. "I am going to call the manager and—"

"Twila! Get this dog of yours girl! Driving me crazy. Barks at everything and everybody!" Her mother yelled. "Now Twila Marie Anderson!"

"Okay, Ma, I'm coming!" *Just put her in the cage or something*, she mumbled under her breath, surely not to say it loud enough for her mother to hear.

"Maddie, Hush!" Her mother fussed through Maddie's loud barks and the screams of the kids outside.

"I will hit you back later Adriana."

"Okay."

Twila ended the call and jumped up off the beanbag. "Maddie!" She called out as she headed down the stairs.

"Girl, what in the world took you so long? You know this dog worries me with all that barking. Why don't you take her out for a walk? Get her out of here and give my head a break."

Twila grabbed Maddie and moved her away from the back door just in time before the kids made their way back around to Twila's house.

"I don't know why she barks so much," Twila laughed.

"I think your father got this dog for you just to annoy me. A Christmas gift for you but the real gift is to him; millions and millions of headaches for me."

"Really ma?" Twila stammered through giggles. "Daddy knew I wanted a dog, so he got me Maddie."

"Yeah right, go and take Maddie out for a while. Give me a break," her mother replied. "What took you so long?"

"I was talking to Adriana," Twila answered as she grabbed Maddie's harness and leash from the coat rack.

"Alright, Twila. Be careful."

"I know, I know but she's better now, Ma."

"Oh really? Let's just hope so. I haven't forgotten how she tried to pull you into all her mess and the acc—"

"Yep, I know ma, but she was sick then. Adriana worked really hard and she's better now," Twila said as she quickly placed her dog in its harness and snapped the leash in place, hurrying before her mother went on an hour-long rant about the dangers of Adriana and all the trouble that can and will follow if she wasn't careful.

CHAPTER 2

Chile, why don't you find something to do? Grab the bags of potato chips out of the car and bring them in here. Always sitting around doing nothing."

Twila shook her head at her grandmother while she was fussing at her cousin. *Grandma is always trippin'. Always fussing at somebody.* Twila chuckled and walked into the kitchen, glad that her mom wasn't in the way, decorating the place like Twila was five instead of seventeen. *That's mommy for you, always being extra.*

"Twila! Come outside with me. I want to show you what I leaned at practice the other day!"

Twila smiled at her seven-year-old cousin. "Okay, let me see what you got." Walking outside, Twila inhaled the relaxing soft breeze that was blowing in the air before taking a seat on the front porch.

"Look Twila!"

"I'm looking Asia. Go ahead and show me what you got!"

Twila laughed at her cousin as she tried to imitate what she had learned from her Coaches at her cheerleading practice. "Keep going! You'll get it."

Asia sat down in the driveway like she'd just lost her one and only friend.

"Dang, they really get all in their feelings about cheers," Twila quipped before she stood up and stretched. "Come on Asia, lets' go and check on Maddie."

"Maddie! Yay!"

Why did I just say that? Now, she is going to want to stay in my room the entire time she's here; Maddie is going to get tired of her real quick. "Yeah, come one," Twila smiled, anxious to get her cousin off the ground before their grandmother came out and started fussing about it.

"Grandma! I'm going to see Maddie!" Asia excitedly yelled while running towards the stairs.

"Oh Lord! Leave that dog alone gal, you know how bad that dog barks. Don't even get that thang started."

Asia ignored her grandmother and trotted up the stairs anyway, rushing straight to Twila's room. Twila laughed when she heard the faint growl followed by a few barks and then cheerful laughter. *Good, Maddie will keep Asia occupied for a little while, so I won't have to pretend her cheers are lit.* Walking into the kitchen, she popped a potato chip in her mouth and looked out the window. The wind rustled a bit harder than it had a few minutes before, causing a rustling of the trees. Looking at the trees but not really looking, her mind resorted to Josh. *Josh,* she mumbled silently as she thought about his strange and at times, erratic behavior. *What the hell is going on with him?* Sighing, she grabbed another chip and walked into the living room. *No need to get a headache thinking about him right now. Let me get grandma stirred up,* she chuckled.

"Was sup grandma?"

Flopping down in the recliner, she flipped the chair up and waited for her grandmother to start conversation, knowing that she was getting herself into more conversation than she wanted to when it came to her grandmother. She always for sure had stories to tell from back in the "good ole days", as she called it.

"Hey baby. Yo' momma still at the store?"

"Yes ma'am. I told her that she didn't have to get a lot of stuff because I am only having a few people over."

"Yeah, well, you know yo' momma. She always has to get stuff even when she doesn't need it. You know, she been like that ever since she was a little girl."

And there it is, Twila chuckled internally. The doorbell rang, stopping the long-winded conversation in its tracks. Smiling at her grandmother, Twila pushed her feet down on the recliner and hopped up. Looking out the window, she saw Adriana standing on the porch. Opening the door and looking glancing at her grandmother, she smiled.

"Hey girl."

"Was sup," Adriana said while playfully pushing Twila and stepping in the house.

"Yo chick, you not gonna believe..." Adriana stopped when she saw Twila's grandmother staring at her as if she was the devil himself. *Girl, why you ain't tell me your grandma was here*, she whispered as quietly as she could.

"How are you doing Ms. Shirley," Adriana said nervously.

Twila eyed her grandmother, hoping that she wouldn't say anything out the way to Adriana. She still had a problem with her due to the accident that happened last year. All that happened last year, and my family is still trippin' about it; just crazy, Twila quipped, careful not to say it loud of enough that her grandmother would hear her. She made that mistake of questioning her grandmother's thought process once when she was younger and got slapped to the floor. Lesson learned; she always thinks before she says something that her grandmother would deem disrespectful.

"Fine."

"Uh, that's good," Adriana answered quickly.

Slightly shaking her head, she pulled Adriana's jacket. "Come on, let's go chill on the porch," Twila suggested before her grandmother jumped in her feelings and cussed Adriana out.

"Girl, your grandmother can't stand me." Adriana sat down on the porch, looking behind her.

"I know, she can't," Twila laughed. "Nah, I'm just playin'. She likes you; she just gets in her feelings a lot. That's all."

"Yeah right, she just don't like me."

Twila sat down on the porch next to Adriana and plucked her in the head before looking out into the street.

"Watch dem' hands," Adriana laughed.

"Whateva chick."

"So, was sup?"

"Nothing, ready to get this gathering over with so I can just chill for the rest of the... oh, I meant to tell you about my dream I had the last night. Girl, we were about to get blown up! I was so glad when I woke up form that crazy dream."

"Wow, I'm glad it was just a dream. I ain't got time for nothing like that. Got too much to do to be dying all early."

"Right," Twila laughed but was quickly met with a quick shutter of her shoulders as she thought of just how real the dream seemed. A little too real.

The girls watched a group of kids form to play a game of hide and seek.

"You count!"

"No! I started the last time! You do it!"

"Kids," Twila chuckled. "Arguing over who starts the game." Looking over at Adriana, she frowned. "Aye. Why the long face all of a sudden?"

Adriana sighed deeply and put her head down. "I still have those nightmares; I just can't get away from them. Now that you said something about your dream...got me thinking all over again."

Twila put her arm around Adriana and smiled. "The good part is that they are only dreams. I shouldn't have said anything about mine. My bad."

"Nah, it's all good. It's not your fault that I killed the—"

"Uh uh...nope, we aren't going to keep talking about it. You have to stop saying it that way. You made a mistake and you paid for it, so we are not going to keep saying it that way."

Good, mommy's back, Twila mumbled as her mother's car pulled up in the driveway. *I hate it when Adriana gets all in her feelings about Kyle and the accident.* Twila shook her head as her mother hopped out of the car as soon as she cut the engine; all excited.

"Hey girls! Ya'll come on in and help out with some more balloons."

"Ma, not more balloons, please. We already have-"

"Hush! And come on so we can get this party started."

"Hey Adriana. How are you doing?"

"Hi Ms. Sharon. I'm ok, how are you doing today?"

"Oh, I can't complain."

Walking into the house, they were greeted by a frustrated Shirley.

"Girl! You took long enough! Where in the world have you been?"

"Hey momma, the store was crowded today. You should've come out there with me; get out of the house for a little while."

"Nope, I was just fine right here. No need for me to be going out in that crowd of people shopping for nothing."

There she goes, Twila shook her head. *One suggestion and we have to hear about why it's a bad idea to go and shop.* Twila laughed and looked at Adriana, a look of pure panic displayed all over her face. "Lighten up girl. Come on so we can get this *party* over and done with."

"Ugh, I just don't like coming over when your grandma is over here. I know she just hate—"

"She does not hate you. Stop worrying so much about my grandmother."

"She does and so does your aunts. Are they coming over—"

"Hey! Hey! Where is the cake?"

"Oh no... Twila, let's go outside."

Twila laughed before calling into the living room to speak to her aunts from her dad's side of the family. "Come on girl, let' just go out the back door." The girls walked out onto the back porch and Adriana sighed a huge sigh of relief. Twila trotted down the stairs and gasped at what she saw. Frowning, she watched Josh closely while he was yelling at some boy; a boy who looked familiar but Twila couldn't place him. *Look at him, acting like a fool again.*

"What is wrong with your man?"

Twila kept her eyes on Josh, not sure if she should just watch or actually do something to stop him from making an even bigger fool of himself. *He really has been acting strange. What is wrong with him?*

"I don't know girl; he's been acting a damn fool." Looking inside her house, she saw her mother walk by, holding a plate of cookies, her aunts behind her. *I hope they don't come out here and see that.* She looked back over at Josh and sighed, opting to stay out if it and hoped that he would snap out of his craziness.

"He better stop runnin' up on people like that. That's Tip and he's in a gang."

"A gang," Twila repeated.

"Yep, and they go for that eye for an eye type stuff. Josh better sit his butt down somewhere talking to him crazy."

Twila sat down on the step and put her head down, hoping that Josh would go home instead of coming over to see her.

CHAPTER 3

"Was sup Twila."

"Hey," Twila spoke to a boy from her social studies class while walking to the bus stop. Twila mainly kept her distance from a lot of the kids who attended her school. Some seemed to have a problem with her because of the accident and the fact that she was still cool with Adriana. To keep herself out of trouble, Twila remained quiet on the bus most days and kept busy reading until the bus reached her school. Standing by herself, her mind wandered to Josh. Maybe he won't be in one of his moods today, she thought. Looking past the crowd of kids, Twila readied herself to get onto the approaching bus. On cue, the bus pulled up in front of them. Twila waited until everybody boarded the bus and she got on after, sitting in the front, directly behind the bus driver.

"Sell out," a girl Twila knew in passing, said loudly. "She should've been up in that place right with her friend."

Twila rolled her eyes and kept her mouth shut.

"Not today!" the bus driver yelled and shook her head. "We not doing this today."

Twila put her ear buds in her ear and turned her music on. Determined to keep her cool from all the kids who wanted to make her life miserable. The kids who blamed her for the reason Kyle wasn't here anymore; wasn't here to win all the football games. Now, our team sucks, they would say. Twila shook her head. They don't care that an innocent person's life was taken, they only care about that fact that he was the one who won football games and put the school on the *map*.

Such losers and lames, she whispered as she focused her attention on her music and the trees passing by.

Buzz... Bzzzz... Bzzz..., Grabbed Twila's attention. She quickly opened her bookbag and retrieved her phone. Smiling, she read the text message from her father.

Skating this weekend...

Love you...

Love you too, ttyl, she typed in. Placing her phone back into her bookbag, she focused her attention back on the music coming out of her earbuds and the scenery passing her by outside.

"Why you not driving with that slut of a friend you got?!" Ebony, one of the wannabee hot girls of the school yelled out, causing an eruption of laughter.

"None of yo' business," Twila shot back, rolling her eyes.

"What?"

"You heard me the first time, wit' your lame self."

"Oh, you tryin' to take it there? We can go there?" Ebony stood up.

"Sit down! The bus driver yelled. I will be writing you up when we get to school, Ebony. I want complete silence on this bus! I'm not playin' with ya'll today!"

The bus got silent with the exception of a few chuckles.

"Don't make me pull this bus over. If I have to do that, all ya'll will be getting write-ups." The bus driver looked around through the rearview mirror, daring anybody to speak.

Twila chuckled and turned her music back on. I cannot wait to get this day over with, she mumbled as the kids on the bus remained eerily quiet. Perhaps, too quiet.

The bus pulled up in front of the school. Twila looked up at the big blue sign that towered over the school's lawn. **Harriet High School**: **Home of the Eagles** read in big bold, red letters.

"Alright, when y'all get on this bus later today, I want silence. We are not riding home with a bunch of nonsense," the bus driver reprimanded while the kids stood to get off the bus. Twila purposely waited until all the kids were off before she stood to exit. Grabbing her book bag, she maneuvered out of the seat and walked off the bus. Sighing, she worked hard to tune out all the noisy kids that were, in her opinion, too old to be acting out like they tended to do every single morning. She looked around for Adriana before she headed inside the school. Standing by the door, her eyes focused on the bench that was just recently painted. The number 23, Kyle's jersey number, was painted in red. A small tree blossomed beside the bench and a beautiful hand painted sign that read, In Memory of Kyle Jones stood proudly in front of the memorial. Twila has seen Kyle's memorial more times than she could count, and each time brought a chill. Her mind always wandered to that fateful, rainy night that changed her life, Adriana's, most of the students, faculty, and staff's lives. Not to mention the detrimental lost to the football team.

"Hey girl! Thanks for waiting. My dad was late picking me up today," Adriana said as she waved goodbye to her father. "He had to work overtime again at his night job."

Twila waved at Adriana's father as he blew his horn. "I told you, I got you." Twila said to Adriana as they entered into the school together. "Just don't pay any attention to these haters. You know how everybody is and they don't even talk about what happened anymore."

Adriana gave Twila the side-eye. "Yeah right. I'm sure they are still talking about how I killed the star."

"No... well, just a few but forget them," Twila thought about the fiasco on the bus earlier and rolled her eyes. "What they think or say don't matter. You will be just fine. It's your first day back after a long vacation. It's understandable to be nervous but you will be ok."

Twila and Adriana walked as calmly as possible through the crowded, noise filled hallway.

"Good Morning, girls."

"Good Morning, Ms. Hanks," Twila and Adriana both said in unison to their principal.

"Welcome back Adriana. Please let me know if there is anything that I can do for you. You know I am always here to help you get back in the swing of things," Ms. Hanks smiled and placed her hand on Adriana's back.

"Thank you, Ms. Hanks," Adriana smiled.

Wow, Twila thought. *The new Adriana; all polite. She was never like this before.*

"You girls have a good day."

"Hey! No running! This is school, not the basketball court or football field," Ms. Hanks yelled at a group of boys running and playing in the halls.

Twila chuckled and walked over to her locker. "Okay, girl. Do your thing with this locker. Nothing's changed. I still can't get this thing open most of the time"

Adriana laughed. "Let's see if I still have the magic touch." Adriana turned the lock clockwise, stopped and looked at Twila. "Okay, watch closely," she said slowly.

"Oh, girl stop it and open the locker," Twila laughed.

Adriana giggled as she finished the rotations to snap the lock open. "Ta-da. Still got it."

"Thanks girl. I missed yo—"

"I called you last night. Why you ain't call me back?" Josh interjected, standing in between the girls.

"Uh, she was busy... maybe."

"I wasn't talking to you, Adriana," Josh quipped. "I was talking to my girl."

"I turned my phone off early, Josh. You know, a quick hello would've been nice before you went in on me," Twila rolled her eyes.

"Whateva," Josh mumbled and walked off.

Twila huffed and slammed her locker shut. "See, I told you he's been acting funny lately. Now watch, later today, he's going to be sweet. I don't know what's wrong with him."

"I told you to just forget him Twila. You can do better."

"Yeah, I guess. Do you want me to walk you to your class? You good?"

"Oh yeah," Adriana responded. "I'm good. I will see you at lunch."

"Okay girl and text me if you need me. We can always do a bathroom call."

Adriana smiled and headed to her class. Twila followed suit, walking towards her first and hardest class of the day. Ms. Engelman's math class.

"Ladies! Let's bring it in. You're moving too slow today! Let's go!"

Twila rolled her eyes at her P.E teacher, Coach Snow. Well her name is Coach Gardner, but the students of Harriet High nicknamed her Coach Snow due to her mop of white hair. Yep, Coach Snow was her name and they went with it; behind her back anyway. "Why is P.E even a requirement," she complained as she jogged on the school's track. Looking over at the houses that lined the street, Twila sighed. *I can't wait to get home.* Taking another long sigh, then, taking a long swig of her bottled water she kept with her during P.E class, she continued with her thoughts of anything but her present location. *I wonder what Maddie is up to right now?* Keeping her mind occupied on anything but the run, she thought more about her dog. *I need to give her a bath today; maybe take her to see daddy.*

"Let's bring it in ladies!"

"Finally!" Twila huffed, picking up speed to make it to the locker room as fast as she could.

Standing in line, Twila winced and shook her head as her P.E teacher yelled her words, even though the class was right in front of her.

"Let's get those feet moving a little faster next time!"

"We are right here," one of the classmates said. "Why is she still yelling?" The girls burst out in laughter as they made their way to the locker room.

"Okay, girls. Let's hit the showers! Bus riders, the buses will be late today, so you have some extra time!"

"Ugh! Why does she always yell?" Twila whispered while opening her locker to retrieve her belongings. *Ha, so much easier than my other locker; opens with ease,* she smiled. *Why can't we just use our own locks with all the lockers here at*

31

this school? Grabbing her bag, she opened it and pulled out her changing clothes and sat down on the blue bench that lined the lockers. *Where did I put my shoes?* Twila rummaged through her bag, seeing everything but her changing sneakers. *Oh, right here.* Pulling the sneakers out of her bag, she placed them on the bench and prepared to take a quick shower before getting on the bus. *I really need to get a car*, she thought as she thought of the noise and the taunting that she faced from the kids who blamed her personally for Kyle's accident. *I will talk to daddy about a car this weekend when we go skating.* Combing through the items in her bag, she looked to make sure she had her deodorant and favorite body spray handy.

"Hey Twila, everything ok? Aren't you going to hit the shower?"

"Uh, yes, Coach Snow, I mean... I'm sorry, Coach Gardner, I was just looking for my shoes. Getting ready to go now."

Coach Gardner laughed aloud, catching Twila by surprise. "Coach Snow, I love it. I know all about my nickname," she laughed. "You kids are funny. You girls just wait until you get my age and have some grey spots on your head. Coach Snow..."

Twila, feeling embarrassed but smiled anyway. "Yeah," she managed to mutter.

"Have a good weekend Twila. See you next week."

"Okay Coach," Twila smiled, remaining quiet until her Coach was out of ear shot. "Oh my gosh! I can't believe I just did that! I cannot believe I called her snow," she laughed. Getting up off the bench, she snatched her bag and headed towards the showers but stopped when she heard a man's voice. Listening closer, she frowned. *This is the girls' locker room. Why is a man in here?*

"Well, you don't have a choice. You either do it or you're off the team," the man's voice muffled.

Twila moved closer to the office's entrance but remained out of view.

"Okay," she heard another voice speak.

"Josh?" She whispered. *What are they doing in here?* Peering through the door, she spotted Josh and Josh's football Coach, Coach Davis. *Why are they in here?*

Come on Josh. Let's get it done before those girls come back through here.

Twila gasped when she saw the needle Coach Davis had in his hand.

"Just a little pinch," she heard him say right before he stuck Josh with it.

CHAPTER 4

"hat's got you so quiet?"

Twila looked up at her father. "Nothing, just thinking," she answered. *What was in that needle and why was Josh's Coach sticking him with it?*

"About what?"

"Uh, just homework," Twila lied. *There is no way that I can tell daddy, the lead detective in this town, about what I saw. He would immediately start an investigation.*

"Oh, okay," her father smiled.

"Twila, you're in for a treat tonight. My specialty spaghetti and meatballs," Candice, Twila's step-mother cheerfully walked in carrying a huge white plastic bowl and sat it on the dining room table.

"Hmmm, looks good," Twila sarcastically replied.

"Twila," her father chastised.

Twila looked over at her father and then back at the food. Taking heave to her father's warning, she smiled. "I love your garlic bread. Did you make some?" Twila looked over at her father, happy to see that he had a smile on his face.

"Girl, I got you," Candice said and sprinted off into the kitchen.

"That's better. Thanks, dumplin'."

Twila flashed her father a fake smile and quickly picked up a cup from the pile her stepmother placed on the table a few minutes before. Looking over at the jugs of drinks, she fixed her eyes on the lemonade. *She tries too hard. We don't need four big pitchers of juice just 'cause I'm here*, Twila silently ranted. *Ugh, why daddy? Why did you marry her?*

"Help yourself dumplin'. There's lemonade, orange juice, grape juice, and Candice's specialty, sweet lemon tea. The tea is really good, try some."

"Oh, I think I will just have some lemonade," Twila said. Grabbing the pitcher of lemonade, she slowly poured the juice into her cup and frowned. Big lemon pieces and bits of seeds poured out and into her cup. "Dang, she can't even make lemonade right."

"Twila!"

"Ooops, did I say that out loud?" Twila chuckled. "Sorry daddy," she said as she looked over towards the kitchen, hoping that Candice didn't hear her. "The last thing I want to do is make the little lady cry," she mumbled.

"Okay, Twila."

Flashing her father another fake smile, she got up from the table, went into the living room and grabbed her book bag. Opening it, she snatched her bag that her mother prepared for her each and every time she visited her father; a survival kit, her mother named it, filled with bottled water, fruit, granola bars and quick snacks. Just a little something for you to survive on while you're there. Lord knows that girl can't cook, and she knows nothing about taking care of kids, Twila heard her mother's voice. *Fred ought to be ashamed of himself. Marrying that twenty-two-year-old child.* Twila chuckled as she thought of her mother and her rants about her father's choices. Putting her book bag back in the corner of the room, she looked over at Maddie's cage. "Still sleeping, I'm shocked," she said while heading back into the dining room. "Oh, the garlic brad smells good," she fibbed. *It smells burnt and I wish she would come on so I can force this meal down my throat and get it over with.*

"Looks good honey," her father said, standing up to move the cups out of the way.

"Twila, I hope you are hungry," Candice smiled.

"Yep, very," Twila answered.

"Okay, y'all dig in."

Twila watched her father take a big spoonful of spaghetti and dab it on his plate. Following suit, she grabbed a piece of garlic bread and placed it on her plate, working hard not to laugh at how hard it was. Next, she grasped the spoon that was sitting in the spaghetti and put a little on her plate.

"That's all you're eating?"

"Uh, yeah. I don't want to get too full. This is enough for me." Twila studied the noodles, mixed with nothing but spaghetti sauce. *This is what she calls her infamous spaghetti. Some noodles drenched in sauce. Ma is right, this lady doesn't know what she's doing.* Twila looked around the table and smiled.

"So dumplin', how's everything going in school?"

The question brought Twila's mind back to Josh and his Coach. *What in the world was going on there?* She quietly asked herself. *Why isn't Josh answering my calls?* "School, everything is good. I'm getting ready to take the final exams soon so studying hard for them."

"That's my girl," her father replied before eating a forkful of his food.

"High School. I remember those days," Candice said while pouring herself some orange juice.

I'm sure you do. It wasn't that long ago. "Oh," Twila replied, careful not to say what she was really thinking.

"How's your mom doing?"

Twila looked at her stepmother like she had five eyes growing from the center of her forehead. "She's doing good." *Why? It's not like you like her.*

"That's good. Please tell her that I said hi when you talk to her."

Twila remained quiet. Instead of responding, she forced the last bit of food into her mouth and swallowed. Thankful that was her last bite, she got up from the table. "Thank you, that was delicious."

"I'm so glad you enjoyed it," Candice gleefully responded.

Twila looked over at her father to make sure she had his approval. She was happy to see the big smile he had etched across his face. *Good, daddy is happy, and I don't have to hear his mouth later. All good.* "I'm going to take Maddie out for a walk daddy."

"Okay, dumplin'. Hurry back. It's supposed to rain soon."

"Okay," Twila called out.

"Are you walking by yourself?" Candice asked. "I can walk with you if you want me to."

"No, it's cool," Twila quipped. "Adriana is going to walk with me."

"Oh, okay," Candice replied. Twila heard a hint of hurt in her voice but kept it moving anyway.

"No time for that," she mumbled.

"Come on Maddie." At the sound of her name, Maddie jumped up and wagged her tail. Opening the cage, Twila flopped down on the floor and giggled as her dog leapt into her arms.

"Hey girl," Twila cooed. "Ready for a walk? Where did I put your leash?" Looking around the living room, the leash was nowhere in sight.

"Daddy?! Have you seen Maddie's leash?"

Where did I put it? Twila chuckled at Maddie, the anxiousness she displayed to go out for a walk. Her little body shivered, and her tail wagged hysterically. "Hold on Mad," Twila giggled. "I have to find your leash."

"Daddy?!"

"It's in your bedroom Twila. I put it in there earlier. Look on the dresser."

"Oh, okay dad."

"Hang on Maddie. I'm coming." Twila ran towards the stairs and reached the first one "Ow!" she winced. "Ouch," she cried and sat down on the second step to rub her ankle. "Why is her shoe sitting on the stairs?" She growled.

"Hey, what's wrong dumplin'?"

"I tripped over Candice's shoe," Twila fussed. "I didn't see it sitting on the stairs. I tripped over the heel and hurt my ankle." Twila looked at the stiletto heel and frowned. "*Ugh*," she spat and rolled her eyes.

"Let me see it. Maybe we should put some ice on it."

"No dad, I'm fine."

Twila looked up to see Candice looking at her with worry and sadness gripping eyes.

Twila forced a smile. "Nice shoes," she uttered, hoping to lighten the mood.

"I'm sorry, Twila. I forgot to put them away earlier."

"It's okay. I'm fine."

"You sure dumplin'? Maybe you should wait a while before you take Maddie out for her walk."

"No, it's fine. Can you go and get her leash for me? My ankle is feeling better now," she said while gently rubbing it.

"Okay dumplin'," her father nodded his head before heading up the stairs.

"Hey Twila, I'm really sorry about this," Candice spoke softly.

Twila snickered. "I should've paid more attention. It's okay. I'm fine. See?" Twila stood up and smirked. "I told you, I'm good."

"Okay, I'm glad you're ok."

There was an awkward pause while the two waited for the leash. Twila sat back down on the step and looked around; she noticed a new picture sitting on one of the end tables that she hadn't noticed before. A picture of her dad and Candice, smiling like they were the only ones in the world who mattered. A twinge of jealously hit Twila's gut but she mentally shook it off.

"Here you go, baby girl."

"Thanks daddy. I better go ahead and get her out for her walk before she burst open!" The family looked over at the tiny dog and laughed as Maddie had already made her way to the door.

"Damn Twila! That dog of yours barks at everything and everybody," Adriana said as she, Twila, and Maddie made their way to the neighborhood park.

"Girl shut up and leave my dog alone. You've been complaining about her the entire walk," Twila laughed. "That's her way of protecting me."

"No, that's her way of being annoying," Adriana giggled. "She's been barking ever since you came to my house and we started this walk."

"Whateva," Twila shot back.

"She is cute though," Adriana smiled.

"Yep, she is."

The girls walked past a group of boys playing football and sat at one of the picnic benches.

"That's all these boys do around here; nothing but football," Adriana commented.

Twila's mind wandered back to what she saw Friday afternoon in the locker room. Picking her dog up and placing her on her lap, she saw the needle go into Josh's thigh and she shuddered at the thought. A strong breeze blew over the park, catching the girls off guard.

"My dad said it was supposed to rain today," Adriana said, snapping Twila out of her grim thoughts.

"Yeah, my dad said that too."

Sitting in silence, both girls gazed at their surroundings while Maddie laid her head on Twila's lap, looking at nothing in particular. Twila especially admired the rose bushes that lined the side of the parking lot.

"So, have you talked to Josh?"

Again, Twila's mind began to wander but she quickly dismissed the thoughts that were forming in her brain. "No, I called him, but he didn't answer," she sighed.

"Oh. So, he's still acting funny?"

"I guess," Twila answered and rubbed the back of her dog's ear. "I guess he will call me back."

Twila fixed her eyes on the small group of joggers coming their way, using them to distract her mind away from Josh. In an instant, Maddie began to bark at the group as they came closer.

"There she goes," Adriana shook her head.

"No, Maddie," Twila said as she tried to pull Maddie's attention away from the women. The women passed and smiled at Maddie as Maddie continued to bark.

"Aw, what a cute dog," one of the women said as she jogged by.

Twila smiled back, happy that they have passed so Maddie could quiet down.

"You have two problems, Twila. Your man and your dog."

"Shut up," Twila replied to Adriana and laughed.

Feeling the vibrations of her phone, Twila maneuvered through her pocket and pulled her phone out. Her mother's picture stared back at her. "Oh," she flatly said. "I was hoping it was Josh," she whispered before answering the call and pushing the speaker button.

"Hi ma."

"Hey girl, I see you're still alive so that woman is doing ok for now."

Twila laughed, "I'm fine ma."

"What did you eat for dinner?"

"Spaghetti."

"You mean some noodles with sauce thrown on top," her mother jabbed.

Twila and Adriana both laughed aloud. "Yeah, something like that," Twila answered.

"Yeah okay. You can always eat something from your survival kit I fixed up for you."

Twila looked at Adriana and shook her head. Adriana chuckled and looked over at the boys playing football.

"I know ma."

"Alright. Well, I'm on my way to the grocery store. You know I have to stock up so when you come home, you can have some real food waiting for you."

"Mommy, Stop. I will call you before I go to bed."

"Okay baby. Love you."

"Love you too ma." Ending her call, Twila looked down at Maddie and then at Adriana.

"Maybe Josh will call you before the night is over," Adriana said, seemingly reading her friend's mind.

"Yeah, maybe," Twila sighed. A cool raindrop hit the top of Twila's forehead. "We'd better go, it's starting to rain."

"Yeah," Adriana agreed.

Putting Maddie down on the ground, Twila stretched. "Come on Maddie."

The girls laughed at Maddie as she excitedly readied herself for more walking time.

CHAPTER 5

Feeling fresh from her shower and rubbing lotion on her legs, Twila looked around at the pink and purple walls. Baby pictures and old elementary school awards crowded her room. *So different than my room at home.* Chuckling, Twila walked over to her closet and opened the door. Finding all of her dolls and their houses stacked up on the top shelf. *Oh daddy, you still have all of this here. I could've sworn he was going to put all this stuff up in the attic. It's not like I'm going to play with them.* I guess, she quipped before closing the door and walking back over to her bed. Flopping down, she grabbed her diary and sighed. *I don't even know if I should write tonight.* Thinking of Josh's words, she threw the diary on the other side of the bed and grabbed her phone. Opening her contacts, she scrolled until she saw Josh's picture. What is up with you? Tapping his face, she listened as the phone rang.

"Twila?"

Ending the call, she looked towards the door. "Yeah?"

"Are you decent? Can I come in?"

Sitting up on her bed, Twila put her phone down. "Yes daddy. Come on in."

Twila smiled as her father walked into the room. "Just wanted to come in and say goodnight. Is everything ok?"

"Yep, all is fine."

"K, good."

Twila eyed her father, wondering why he was sitting there looking like he'd just lost his best friend. "Um, okay. I guess I will get ready to go to sleep now dad."

"Listen Dumplin', I know you don't like Candice, but I am hoping that you try to get along with her. I know you blame her for your mom and I splitting up and getting a divorce but—"

"No daddy, I never said that I didn't like her. It's just she's—"

"You don't have to say it. It's all in your actions baby girl. I see how you act when she's around."

Twila heard the faint buzzing of her phone and turned her attention to it. As she hoped, Josh's face displayed boldly on the screen. Keeping her contentment hidden, she looked back at her father as he continued his chat. "You know, she's a good woman and I'm happy so I am hoping that the two of you can come together and make some type of truce. Maybe you too can go shopping or grab—"

"Okay, dad. I got it. I will try to be nicer." Twila waited impatiently, hoping the "play nice" comment would get her father out of the room so she could call Josh back.

"Thanks, dumplin'. I really appreciate it."

Shifting her weight, Twila reached up and hugged her father. *Throw in a hug and that would really get him going.*

"What's that for?"

"Well, because you're my daddy and I love you."

"My baby. I love you too dumplin'. Get some rest and I will see you in the morning."

Twila planed a big smile on her face as she watched her dad give Maddie a quick rub and head out the door.

"Finally!" Laying back on her bed, she picked up her phone and made the call that she has been dying to make.

"Hello?"

"Josh."

"Yeah, was sup?"

"You tell me. What is really going on with you?"

"What do you mean? I was sleep when you called earlier. I saw that you called so I called you back."

Twila looked over at Maddie, then back at Josh. "That's not what I'm talking about and you know it. I mean with everything. You've been so distant over the past few days and when we do talk, you're mean to me."

"Twila. I'm not in the mood. I'ma go back to sleep. I'll hit you back tomorrow."

"Josh, wait. I'm sorry. I'm just worried about you. That's all."

"Well, there's nothing to be worried about."

Twila paused for a brief second to give her mind time to think about something lighter to chat about. *Ariel*, she, thought. "How's Ariel? It's been a while since I've seen her."

"Ariel?"

"Yeah, your little sister," Twila chuckled. Hoping a conversation about family would lighten his mood.

"Yeah, she good."

"Good. Tell her that I said hi and I will visit her soon."

"Yeah, okay. I think my mom is going to ask you to babysit anyway so you can see her then."

"Oh, okay." *Bingo, it worked. Josh sounds so much better.*

"Okay, cool."

"So, you want to go to the movies or something next week?"

"Yeah, sure. I would love to go. It's been a minute since we've been out on a date."

"Yeah, it has," Josh responded with a yawn. "Well, I'm going to go back to sleep. I will come by and see you tomorrow. Where you at? At your pop's crib?"

"Yep, I will be going home tomorrow night."

"A'ight, I will just wait until you get home and stop by after practice."

"Okay."

"A'ight."

Twila kept her eyes on the phone a little longer than needed after Josh had hung up. "Huh," she muttered and placed her phone on the nightstand. Looking over at Maddie again, she smiled.

"Goodnight, Maddie." Maddie looked over at Twila and then put her head down. Twila chuckled, turned her lamp off and prepared herself for a restful night's sleep.

Opening her eyes, Twila looked over at her phone. *2:42 A.M.* sparkled in blue along with some social media notifications. Sitting up, she tossed the blankets and sheets over to the side and slid her feet to the floor. Yawning, she got up and walked out her room, using the faint light from the bathroom's nightlight to guide her through, she tip-toed down the stairs and into the kitchen.

Mouth is too dry. Going to the fridge, she looked around at her choices and frowned.

Definitely don't want none of that nasty lemonade. Setting her eyes on a carton of milk, she grabbed it and closed the refrigerator. Opening the cabinet, she got a glass, and quickly poured some milk into it. Taking a small sip of her drink, she surveyed her surroundings.

That's something her and my mom have in common; plants. So many plants over here and at home. Too many. Gulping the rest of her milk, she rinsed the glass out in the sink, placed it on the counter, and walked back up the stairs and got back into bed. Hoping that this time, when she awakes, it would almost be time for her to go home.

CHAPTER 6

"Look Twila!"

Twila looked up from her book and giggled. "I see! Keep going! You got it!"

"Ariel couldn't wait until you got here so she can show you that she can ride her big girl bike."

"Not too fast Ariel! Take your time!"

"Okay mommy!"

Twila laughed as Ariel briefly removed both her hands but quickly placed them back on the handlebars when her mother gave her the look.

"So, how are you doing? It's been a while since you've been over here."

Twila put her book down on the porch and smiled. "All is ok, Ms. Trina," she answered.

"Good. How about your friend?"

"Adriana?"

"Yes, how is she doing? I heard that she went off to a treatment facility after the accident."

"Yes ma'am, she did and she's doing a lot better now."

"Well, that's good. I'm happy that she got some help."

"Yeah."

"I better get going. I won't be gone long. As always, you help yourself to anything in the refrigerator. Oh, and there's a fresh bag of popcorn in the cabinet. Please help yourself to as much as you want."

"Okay, thanks," Twila replied and giggled at Ariel as she removed her hands again from the handlebars.

"Ariel!"

"Sorry, mommy."

"That girl is a mess," Trina chuckled. "Where did I put those keys? Chile, here they are. Right here in my face," Trina laughed and shook her head. "If it was a snake, it would've bit me! A saying my momma used to say."

Twila giggled.

"Okay, let me get going. Josh should be home soon."

The mention of Josh's name sparked waves in the pit of Twila's stomach. *Should I ask Ms. Trina about Josh's mood? If anyone should know anything, it has to be his mom.* Standing up, Twila made the notion to call out to Trina and voice her concerns but quickly sat back down. *Nah, he would be so mad at me if I asked his mother about anything.* Twila waved at Trina as she pulled slowly out of the driveway, stopping to kiss her daughter on the cheek before she slowly accelerated onto the street.

"I thought she would never leave!"

Twila turned towards the side of the porch to see Adriana standing there. "What are you doing here?"

"Just thought I'd come keep you and the brat company."

"First of all, she is not a brat! Stop saying that," Twila giggled. "Second, why did you wait until Ms. Trina was gone before you—?"

"'Cause, I'm not ready to face everybody yet. It's bad enough that I have to go to school every day. I am trying to avoid as many people as possible and that included Ms. Trina."

"Twila! Can I ride down there?!"

"No, you have to stay over here!"

"Aw man!"

"That's the rule."

"Oh-kayyy."

Twila smiled at Ariel and then turned back to Adriana. "I guess I can understand that... Adriana?! What is that?!"

"What? This?"

Twila gasped as Adriana pulled a brown paper bag out of her jacket pocket. "No, Adriana! Please don't tell me you—"

"Chill girl, "Adriana laughed. "It's just soda, see."

Twila sighed a deep sigh of relief when she saw that Adriana only had a bottle of soda in the bag. "Girl, you scared me."

Adriana chuckled. "Twila, those days are over. I have learned my lesson."

"Good, I'm glad."

Adriana laughed before taking a long swig of her drink.

"Well, I guess we better go in. Mosquitos are crazy out here. "Ariel! Come on, time to go in!"

"Okay, I'ma go and head on home. I will call you later."

"A'ight, are you sure you don't want to come in? We can sit and have a good girl chat after I get Ariel in front of some cartoons."

"Nah, I better go. I don't want that brat telling her mom I was all up in the house."

"Bye Adriana!" Twila laughed.

"See ya, girl!"

Twila watched Adriana slip out of view before calling Ariel in for the night.

"Ari..." never mind. It won't hurt us to stay out here a little while longer. Sitting back down on the steps, Twila observed her surroundings, catching a glimpse of Josh's football lying on the side of the porch. "Josh," she whispered. I need to find out—"

"Twila! Look!"

"Ariel, girl, stop taking your hands off," Twila laughed. "Your mom is going to get you!" Shaking her head, she looked back over towards the football.

"Sup, Twila."

"Hey," Twila said to a group of boys from the neighborhood as they walked by.

"Where Josh at?"

Good Question. "At practice."

"Dat's was sup. Tell him I said wut up?"

Twila nodded and turned her attention back on Ariel. *I think she had enough.* "Ariel, come on! Time to go in!"

"Aww. Do we have to go in now? Can I go around one more time?"

"Ariel."

"Pleaseeee?"

"Okay, just one more time and then we need to go in."

"Yay! Okay!"

Adjusting her weight, Twila's mind wandered back to Josh. *"Oh well, nothing I can do about how he's acting."* Looking down at her phone, she grabbed it and sat it back down. *"No need, he probably won't even answer."*

"Ow!"

"Ariel?! Oh no! Are you ok?"

"Ow! My knee!"

Running over to Ariel, Twila squatted down and grabbed Ariel's leg. "Aw, it's ok," she said tenderly. "Come on, let's go in."

"It's bleeding!"

"I know, but it's ok. Let's go and clean it up."

"Can you fix it?"

Twila smiled at Ariel and cupped her hand. "Yep, I sure can. Come on. Let me show you."

"Wait!"

"What is it?"

"My bike!"

"Don't worry about your bike. I will come back out and get it after I fix your boo-boo. Okay?"

"Okay."

Twila and Ariel quickly walked up the steps and into the house, closing the door behind them.

"Hurry, the bleeding is going to fall on the floor."

Twila chuckled. "I promise, it's not going to fall on the floor. Let's go upstairs so I can fix it for you. Come on."

Walking up the stairs, Twila gave a reassuring smile. "It's all ok, I promise."

"K," Ariel whispered.

"Go ahead and sit down while I get the alcohol."

"Noooo!"

"What? What's wrong?"

"Alcohol! That will... that will make it hurt."

"Ariel, I promise that I am not going to hurt you. Sit down so I can fix it for you."

"Do you promise it won't hurt?"

"Yes. I promise. Tell you what, if you sit still while I fix it, I will let you have some ice cream."

"Yes!"

"Okay, ice cream is all it takes," Twila laughed.

Preparing her materials, Twila smiled at Ariel and began to fix her boo-boo.

"I don't want any of you talking to anyone about our team! Got it?!"

Josh shook his head but remained quiet.

"You all will be sorry if we don't win this next game! We have a solution to keep winning but some of you are being babies! Don't want to take one for the team. Well let me help you with that! Either you cooperate or I will cut you! Got that!"

Josh looked around at his teammates, knowing that they were all thinking the same exact thing he was thinking. *It's not right but it has to be done*, looks posted on all their faces.

"You have to remember that we are doing this for the team. No need to tell anybody. Not even your parents. Understood?" Josh locked eyes with his Coach before putting his head down.

"More please!" Ariel squealed.

Twila giggled. "I think that is all for now. How about a movie? How does Buster sound?"

"Okayyy."

"Just okayyy? I know how much you love that movie!"

"Yea."

"I know! Come on, I will turn it on for you." Walking through the hallway, Twila glanced at Josh's room before heading into Ariel's. "Okay, let's get this party started!" Grabbing the remote and flipping the TV on, Twila quickly tapped the DVR button to begin the movie. "A'ight, I will be downstairs studying if you need me."

"K."

Twila waited at the door while Ariel settled onto her bed. "Finally," she quipped, as she turned and entered into the hallway. Focusing her attention to Josh's ajar door, she stopped. *Should I? No, sneaking around in your boyfriend's room is not cool. Well, he is my boyfriend... Nah.*

Moving down the hall, she anxiously felt the need to go into Josh's room for answers. *The answers to why Josh is acting all weird could be right in there.* Giving in to her feelings, she whipped past the bathroom and Josh's mom's room to enter his. Walking in, she positioned the door back to its rightful place and uneasily looked around. Looking over at a pile of clothes lying on the floor, she frowned.

"Really Josh? You really need to clean up in here." Planting her eyes on his dresser, she smiled when she saw the picture of him and her that they've taken at the photo booth in the mall. "Oh, so you did keep that picture; sweet." Turning her attention to the task at hand, she moved around slowly and continued to look around. *Think Twila. Think of some good hiding spaces.* Turning to give the other side of the room a scan, she focused her attention on his bed and noticed boxes underneath it.

"What's going on, Josh?" She whispered while walking over to the boxes. Looking over at the door, she sat down on the floor and pulled one of the boxes out of its spot. Taking another peak towards the door, she began to feel flushed and hot all over but continued anyway. Looking through the box, she found pictures of Josh with friends; mainly Kyle. Twila's heart sank when she looked at Kyle's face, his smile. Leaning back against the bed, she sighed and placed the pictures back into the box. Pushing the box back underneath the bed, she proceeded to pull the second box out and placed it in front of her. Nervously, she looked over at the door again and inhaled deeply. Opening the box, she gasped.

"All there is to know about Steroids," she read silently. "Oh no... Steroids."

CHAPTER 7

Twila pushed her stuffed animals over on the other side of her bed and focused her attention on her lap top screen. High school... No, maybe I should go with... Athletes... and... *Athletes and drug use*, she typed. Loads of information popped up swiftly on the screen. Combing through the list, she opened the first story about teens and drug use. Just like many times before, the image of Josh being stuck with the needle pierced her mind which caused her to search harder through the information that displayed on the tiny screen. Illegal and dangerous, she read aloud right before her mother knocked on the door and barged in.

"Hey, what are you up to?"

"Uh, just reading," she said, slamming her laptop shut.

"Uh oh, I'm guessing it's something you don't want me to see. Since you slammed your computer down as soon as I walked in."

Twila put her laptop down beside her and picked up her stuffed animal, placing it on her lap. "No, ma, nothing like that," she chuckled. "Just looking up something for school."

"For school?"

"Yeah ma, school."

"Uh huh. I see," her mother replied while smoothing the comforter on the bed. "So, what's going on with you and Josh? Anything new?"

There it is, Twila thought. *Always all up in my business with me and Josh.* "Josh? Huh? Uh, Josh is good."

"Yeah?" Her mother asked in a full voice full uncertainty and sat down beside Twila.

"Yep, all good."

"Well, he hasn't been by the house lately. What's good with that?"

"Ha! What's good? Ma? Really?"

"Oh, you know, just trying to keep it real."

"Ma, no, stop," Twila laughed aloud.

"What?"

"You not even saying it right," Twila quipped.

"Okay, Alright. Well, I still want to know what's going on. Something isn't quite right. I haven't seen him in a while."

"I guess he's just been busy. You know with football. The season is over, but they still practice. Then he watches Ariel while his mom is at school."

"Why? I thought you were doing that for her?"

"I don't know, I guess she wants to save money or something. I was doing it because Josh had games. Now he's free so it's just easier for her."

"Uh huh. Maybe I will call Trina and see how she's doing."

"Mommy…"

"Okay, okay, I will leave it alone."

A clap of thunder rang, followed by big raindrops, startling them both. Twila shook her head as Maddie began to bark.

"That dog barks at everything," her mother said before standing up and closing Twila's window. "It is really coming down out there. I didn't know it was supposed to rain again today."

"Me either," Twila replied.

"How's pizza for dinner? Crust started delivering."

"Dat's was sup," Twila smiled at her mother.

"Oh, so that's how I'm supposed to say it?"

Twila laughed and hopped off her bed. "Yep, something like that. You're too proper with it."

"Oh, I see. So— Maddie! Stop all that barking!"

Maddie paused, growled lightly and resorted back to her barking with full force.

"Ma, she's going to bark, and she has no idea what you're saying when you tell her to stop," Twila laughed loudly.

"Yeah, well she better learn. I'm telling you Twila, I believe your dad got her only to annoy me."

Twila shook her head, grabbed her phone off the dresser, and walked behind her mother out the bedroom and down the stairs, "Okay ma," she muttered.

"It's okay, Maddie. It's only a storm," Twila said to her dog as she walked into the living room. Opening the cage, she picked her up and sat down on the couch, placing her snuggly on her lap.

"What do you want on your pizza?"

"Pepperoni is fine and whatever you want on it."

Twila watched her mother as she looked through the stack of coupons. *Should I tell her,* she thought to herself. *Maybe she can help me figure out what Josh and his Coach was doing.* Twila stroked Maddie gently and looked out the window at the rain. Putting Maddie on the floor, she walked over to the door and opened it, Maddie stood beside her. *Nah, she would start a whole mess if I was to tell her what I saw. Then daddy would find out somehow and we all would be in trouble.* A strike of lightening pierced through the sky followed by a hefty clap of thunder. On cue, Maddie began to bark loudly. "Oh Maddie," Twila said as she picked her up and walked back over to the couch. "It's just thunder," she smiled. "It's ok."

"Delivery," she heard her mother say. "Yes, that's right, delivery please."

Twila closed her eyes and tuned her mother's phone conversation out as she thought of Josh. *Maybe I should call him back.* Reaching over to get her phone off the other side of the chair, she pushed Josh's number and waited. Four rings and then to voicemail. *Where is he?* I have to get my mind off of him. Spotting one of Maddie's toys on the side of the couch, she grabbed it and threw it across the room.

"Go get it girl," she squealed. Maddie happily ran after her toy, tripping over the carpet.

"Watch where you're going, Mad," she laughed. She watched Maddie lie on the floor and chew her toy. Smiling, her mind quickly reverted back to Josh. "Ugh, I can't get him off my mind," she sighed. *Where in the world is he?* Looking over at her phone, she picked it up and looked through her call list. Searching the list, she stopped when she reached Josh's mom's number. "Ms. Trina," she recited. Maybe she can tell me where he is. Pushing the button, she listened to the phone ring one time and quickly tapped the off button. "Too desperate," she whispered. *I shouldn't be calling his mother, looking for him. Let it go, Twila.*

"Okay, Pizza's on the way."

"Okay."

Twila laughed at Maddie as she lunged at her mother.

"Hey girl, why are you so noisy," her mother said to Maddie as she leapt into her lap." You are cute but too much noise."

Twila smiled at her mother and her dog. "That's her way of protecting us, Ma."

"Yeah, right," her mother replied. "That rain is really pouring."

"Yeah, it is," Twila agreed. Twila looked over at her phone and realized that it was ringing. Josh displayed boldly on the screen. "Josh," she whispered. "Ma, I'll be right back," she said before running up the stairs. Tapping the phone to answer, she reached her room, closed the door and frowned.

"Josh, where have you been? I've been calling you all weekend! What's going on?" Twila looked at her phone. "Josh?"

"Yeah, I'm here."

"Why aren't you saying anything?"

"Uh, because you won't let me say anything. Are you done?"

"Don't play with me, Josh. What is going on?"

"Nothing, I've just been busy, that's all. What are you doing?"

"Really? That's it? You've been busy?"

"Yep. Been busy."

Tiny scratches pulled Twila's attention from the awkward call with Josh. Looking over at her door, she quickly walked over to it and opened it. Maddie walked in slowly and jumped up on the beanbag, licking her paw.

"Josh?"

"Twila. I told you that I was busy. Everything is all good now. So, do you want to go to the movies?"

Twila shook her head in disbelief. "What is wrong with you? You don't answer any of my calls. You disappear for a few days and when I see you, you're in the *girls'* locker room with your coa—"

"What?"

Twila huffed and briefly closed her eyes, not sure if she should continue with the conversation. Her mind wandered back to the moment she saw Josh being injected with the needle.

"What? The girls' locker room?"

Twila noticed Josh's voice change; an irritated yet tender tone.

"What do you know about that Twila?"

"Uh, nothing," she swiftly responded. "I just saw you and your coach standing there. I—"

"Listen to me and listen good. Don't you ever bring that up again! Do you hear me Twila?! Leave that alone. Whatever you saw... you need to forget it."

Twila was dumbfounded when she realized that Josh had abruptly ended the call.

CHAPTER 8

I hate coming to this store," Adriana said while throwing a can of her father's favorite coffee in the shopping cart before frowning at the list of items on her phone that her father asked her to pick up.

Twila chuckled. "Why? What's so wrong with this store?"

Twila and Adriana walked around to the paper products aisle and stopped.

"These people are always following you around; always walking up close. I hate that."

"So, just ignore them," Twila responded while fingering some of the products on the shelf.

"Why do you always do that," Adriana laughed and smacked Twila's hand down.

"I don't know why I always have to touch stuff," Twila laughed.

"You always got your hands on something."

"I know."

The girls walked further down the aisle, Adriana looked through her list again and grabbed a pack of paper plates and threw them into the cart. "I don't know why my dad can't come here and get everything himself."

"Because he works."

"Yeah, but what does that have to do with me? I guess I shouldn't complain. Going to the market for him is the only way that he will let me use his car."

Twila shook her head and found more items to finger.

"I wish my mom and dad would just get back together already so I can go back to doing what I want to do. My mom used to come to this store all the time and keep everything stacked. Now that she moved out, I have to come over here and deal with these people."

"Adriana?" Twila laughed. "What is so wrong with the people here? You are talking about people who work here, right?"

"Yes!"

"Dang! Okay," Twila said and playfully pushed Adriana.

"Like, it's this one boy who, every time he sees me, he has to follow me around. He be actin' like he just working but I know that he walks around just so he can see me." Adriana picked up a stack of paper cups and moved along to the other side.

"So, who is it?"

"I don't know his name and he don't go to Harriet, so I don't know."

"Huh. Does he say anything to you?"

"Sometimes... Sometimes he will speak and that's it but then everywhere I turn in here, I see him. So annoying."

Hmmm, Twila mumbled and shrugged her shoulders. Walking out of the paper products aisle and into the main area of the store, Twila laughed at Adriana while she gave one of the workers are hard glance and then rolled her eyes.

"That must be him."

"Yeah, see how he keeps staring at me?"

"He probably just thinks you're cute and want your number or something," Twila chuckled.

"Humph, yeah right. You know that ain't going down."

"I guess," Twila said.

"Look at those chicks. I should smack one of them."

Twila and Adriana both looked towards the sound of the voice.

"Keep walking Adriana, come on."

"Yo, Adriana! So, you don't mess with us like that anymore?"

"Come on A, let's just keep going."

Adriana and Twila both ignored the biggest bully that attended Harriet High, Torri, and the one who undoubtedly introduced Adriana to her ways that landed her in Holly Grove.

"Oh, it's like that?"

"What do you want Torri?!" Adriana yelled. Twila looked around and spotted two older men staring at Adriana and shaking their heads. Rolling her eyes at the men, Twila turned her attention back to Adriana and gently pulled her arm. "Let's just go girl. You know Torri don't want nothing but to start something."

"I was just saying was sup," Torri responded in a voice that wasn't at all friendly.

"Okay, you said it so now I'm saying goodbye!" Adriana shot back. The group of girls who were with Torri giggled and chuckled.

"Oh, so now you tryin' to play me?"

Adriana rolled her eyes at Torri and then swiftly walked away, leaving her cart behind.

Twila followed suit after she grabbed the cart, jogging a bit to catch up to Adriana.

"What is she even doing here anyways?" Ariana quipped.

"I don't know, and we don't care. Do you have anything else on your list?" The girls stopped while Adriana looked through her phone. "Nah, I think I got everything."

"A'ight cool so let's go ahead and get up out of here." Without saying another word, Twila and Adriana both walked towards the front of the store, desperate to get out of there and to stay out of trouble. Thoughts of the fight she'd had with Torri last year invaded her mind; a fight that happened because Torri had Adriana acting all crazy and as Adriana's true best friend, Twila had to do something to get her away from Torri and her click, girls' who meant her no good and only wanted to corrupt her mind. *I don't feel like dealing with that crazy chick*, she ranted internally.

"What is taking these people so long?"

The shoppers Adriana were referring to both looked at her and rolled their eyes. Adriana rolled her eyes back at them and sucked her teeth in frustration. Twila shook her head and turned, just to look around to pass the time. She spotted Torri in her peripheral, standing with her arms crossed, her girls stood behind her. Turing away from them, she helped Adriana place her groceries on the conveyer belt, working to ignore the trouble that stood behind them. Grabbing a magazine, Twila sighed, hoping that Torri and her girls would behave themselves and just shop or better yet, leave.

"It's about time," Adriana huffed, glad it was finally her turn to pay for her items.

Twila continued to scan the magazine, looking at nothing in general while the cashier scanned the items. Twila chuckled at Adriana while she gave the cashier all types of unnecessary attitude. Putting the magazine back on the rack, Twila walked ahead of Adriana and walked outside. Looking around the parking lot, she spotted Torri again, looking like she was ready to strangle someone. *Why does she keep popping up?* Rolling her eyes, she walked over to Adriana's father's car and leaned up against the trunk, wishing Adriana would hurry. *Finally*! Adriana walked out of the store with the shopping cart and walked over towards the car.

"Hey!" Torri yelled. Adriana let go of the shopping cart and walked towards Torri and her crew.

"No Adriana," Twila whispered. "Adriana!" She called out but it was too late. Adriana smacked the contents out of Torri's hand and the next thing, they were tussling.

"Oh shit! Hey! Stop!" Twila yelled while running over to the fight. The girls kept going with Torri's friends egging them on. "Adriana! Let her go!" Pulling Adriana away from Torri, Twila pushed her over to the side. "Girl, stop! She ain't worth the trouble, believe me!"

"Mind yo' business!" Torri yelled.

"Adriana is my business and you better go ahead somewhere before I whoop yo' ass again. Don't forget about last year!"

"Come on A. Let's go."

"Hey, Hey, Hey! Y'all get away from this store with all that," one of the cashier's ran out of the store and yelled, startling the group. "If you don't leave right now, I will call the police and have all of y'all in jail!"

"Come on Adriana; let's go," Twila said while gently pulling on Adriana's shirt. "We don't need this. They just mad because you don't mess with them like that anymore. That's all."

"Mad! Girl don't nobody care about her!"

"Yeah right!" Twila yelled.

"Alright! Y'all go before I call!"

Adriana turned and smacked her lips at the cashier.

"Oh no, not him," Adriana quipped.

"Hold up Angie! I saw the whole thing. Those girls were messin' with them," the boy who Adriana claimed followed her all around the store ran out and called Torri and her group out. "They always starting something."

"Shut up!" Torri yelled.

"Damon, what are you talking about?"

"Angie, check their pockets."

Everybody had their eyes fixed on Torri.

"What!" Torri shrieked.

Twila glanced at the cars that were slowly driving by, most likely being nosey to what was going on.

"Damon, go in the store and get Charley."

"Okay."

Twila smirked at the look on Torri's face; a look of horror and at the same time, pure disgust.

"Come on y'all. They trippin'," Torri said.

"Yeah, I bet you ready to go now, huh Torri," Adriana laughed.

Twila giggled while Torri, along with her girls, trotted out of the parking lot and out into the streets.

"Girl, how in the world did you get hooked up with Torri?" Twila chuckled.

"I don't know, I guess I just—"

"Hey."

"*Oh damn,*" Adriana mumbled under her breath.

"Adriana!" Twila fumed.

"How are you doing?"

"I'm good. I just wanted to come and introduce myself. My name's Damon."

"Hi Damon. Now bye Damon," Adriana sarcastically said while fumbling with her dad's car keys.

"My name is Twila and that's Adriana."

"Nice to meet you both. I've been—"

Squeals and loud sirens interrupted Damon.

Twila gasped, Adriana laughed hysterically, and Damon just stared straight faced while the police approached Torri. In an instant, Torri and her group were being placed in handcuffs.

"They finally got her," Damon chuckled. "She's been stealing from here for months."

"Wow," Twila mumbled. Her mind immediately reverted back to when Adriana had her problems. "Torri needs to get her life together," she mumbled.

"Yeah, she needs to do something. Come on Twila lets go. Damon, it was nice to meet you."

"Hold up, can I get your number. Maybe call you sometimes."

"I don't think so," Adriana quipped and then hopped in the car.

Twila shrugged her shoulders and smiled at Damon. "Nice to meet you," she said before she followed Adriana's lead and got in on the passenger side.

CHAPTER 9

What in the world is wrong with you?! You love my strawberry cake and now you're sitting there like that big ole piece is not in front of you. What's going on?"

Twila dabbed her fork in and out of her dessert and then shifted her fork up and down before putting it down all together. "Nothing, Ma. I just have a lot on my mind, that's all."

"Oh boy. Who is it this time? Josh or Adriana?"

Twila picked her fork up again and took a bite of her mother's infamous strawberry short cake, just to keep the peace and to keep her mother from her blabbering questions. "It's nothing," she lied. "Just a project I have coming up at school."

"Huh," her mother quipped as she got up from the table.

School always works. Just mention school and she is immediately off my back.

"Oh yea, I meant to tell you to call your father."

"Oh no! Why?" *I really don't want to talk to daddy. My police officer daddy... My detective daddy!* Her mind screamed.

"What do you mean, *why*? He's your dad, Twila. He doesn't need a reason to want to talk to you."

Twila's mind was full of reasons why he would want to talk to her and none of them included just quality daddy and daughter time. "A'ight, ma. I was just asking." Twila got up from the table and glanced at her mother.

"Don't get cute girl and make sure you wash that plate."

"Yes ma'am," Twila said while slowly walking over to the sink and turning the water on. Washing her plate, Josh entered her mind, again. *What is the matter with him*? Twila thought silently as she washed the dish a second time, trying to stay occupied so that her mother would stay out of her business. Trying not to seem too obvious, she grabbed two glasses from the dish rack and cleaned them.

"Can't wash the same dish over and over," Twila chuckled.

"Huh?"

"Um, nothing ma. I was just singing a song."

"Oh okay. Hey, don't forget to stop by Shannon's house today when you take Maddie out for her walk. I told her that you would stop by to pick up the books that she's letting me borrow today."

"A'ight, I will."

"A'ight?"

Twila laughed, "Okay. Is that better?"

"Girl don't make me pop you," her mother laughed.

Twila chuckled and put the two glasses back in its rightful spot on the dish rack. Thoughts of Josh continued to invade her mind. *Steroids, humph. I know that fool is not into steroids.* Twila fumbled around with the glass once more while thinking of what Josh may or may not be doing. *Maybe he has a school project. Yeah, a project for school is exactly what it is. But Josh never does research for anything, why would he start now? Okay now Twila, think girl,* her inner voice screamed at her. Trying to shake the thoughts out of her head, she grabbed a fork from the dish holder and quickly re-washed it. *Whatever you saw...you need to forget it,* she heard Josh's voice take over and become lead within her mind.

CHAPTER 10

"Twila, you are such a sweetheart! Thank you!"

"You're welcome Ms. Trina. I don't have anything else to do tonight. I hope you enjoy yourself."

"Thanks. It's been so long since I've been out with my girlfriends; so busy with school and taking care of Ariel. Then...a lot going on with Josh... you know, all that stuff with Kyle and all. I don't think he's fully over all of that."

"Yeah," Twila muttered.

"You and Josh still dating and all, right?"

Twila shifted in her seat. "Yes, he's cool."

"Have you noticed anything different about him since his friend passed? I know the usual grieving but what about something more than just grieving."

Curiously, she thought silently. "Um, nope. Just missing his friend."

"Yeah, maybe that's all it is," Trina said while adjusting her earrings. "Well! How do I look?" Trina surveyed herself in the mirror while glancing at Twila.

"You look pretty," Twila smiled.

"You sure the choker isn't too much?"

"Nope, I promise, you are fine."

"Okay, well. As always, help yourself to anything in here and I promise to be back before it gets too late."

"Okay, take your time." Twila smiled at Trina and followed her out of the bathroom and into the living room. "Oh yea, it's some chocolate chip cookies on the counter if you want some. Please enjoy; eat as much as you want."

"Thanks," Twila called out and sat down on her favorite chair. Listening to Trina's car start, Twila felt a sense of uneasiness. Torri knows address; she knows how to keep people quiet. Well. At least that's what people at school always say about her. Thoughts of Adriana and Torri's fight filled Twila's mind. Yes, Torri went to jail the other day at the grocery store, but she was quickly let out by her cousin. The feeling of freedom didn't last long at all. Sighing, she walked over to the front door to make sure it was locked. Proceeding to the kitchen, more thoughts of Torri and her gang invaded Twila's thoughts as she twisted the back-door lock to be sure that it was locked completely. *They ain't goin' do nothing*, she said aloud. *Just a bunch of girls with a lot of mouth.* Looking at the window, she made sure the lock was turned the correct way and then headed back to the living room. Slumping down on the couch, she pulled her phone out of her pocket and hit her mother's picture. Listening to the ringing phone, she looked towards the stairs and thought of Ariel. *I will check on her in a sec.*

"Hey baby."

"Hey ma. Whatchu doing?"

Just sitting her watching the news. Everything ok?

"Yeah," Twila sighed. "All is ok. Just wanted to call and see what you were doing."

"Well, you don't sound like you're ok. What's up?"

"It's nothing, just being here by myself is a little creepy tonight, I guess," she answered while looking over at the big window that lined the front of the living room. "It's too quiet in here."

"Oh, I see. Everything is ok. When you feel uneasy, call and talk to me."

Twila chuckled, "Okay mama. I guess I will do some studying. I will call you in a little while."

"Okay and how are you getting home?"

"Ms. Trina said that she will drop me off."

"Alright. I will see you when you get home or if you need me before then, I'm just a phone call away. Love you."

"Love you too ma." Twila responded and ended the call. Feeling a bit more comfortable, she stood, stretched, and headed towards the stairs. Walking past the bathroom, she jumped and yelped. *Oh my gosh! Twila! Calm down*, she scolded herself as she realized her own reflection in the bathroom mirror was the culprit who scared her half to death. Holding her chest and leaning against the stair banister, she laughed. *What is wrong with me?* She quipped, feeling embarrassed and glad no one was around to witness her scaring her own self. Steadying herself, she slowly walked up the stairs, hoping that her incident didn't interrupt Ariel's nap. *I can't believe she is still sleeping, it's only six o'clock.* Opening Ariel's door, she smiled at sleeping Ariel. Maybe I should wake her up... Nah, she can sleep it out, she muttered before closing her door. Walking away, she turned back towards

Ariel's room and opened her door, leaving it ajar before walking back the stairs and heading back down to the living room. Looking around, she sighed and flopped back down on the couch. Pulling her book out of her backpack, she looked at it and threw it on the table, deciding to prop her feet up on the couch and close her eyes instead.

"Huh," Twila said and wiped the sleep from her eyes and the slobber from her mouth.

"I'm back love," Trina chuckled. "You must've been tired 'cause you were sleeping so good!"

Twila stretched and moved her legs off the couch. "Yes, I was. I've been studying a lot at night and haven't had much sleep."

"Well, good. I'm glad you're studying hard, but sleep is important too."

"That's what my mom says too."

"That's because she's a good mom," Trina smiled while taking her earrings off. I want to thank you again for coming over and watching Ariel for me so I can go out for a little while.

"Oh, no problem. Glad I could help."

"Hi mommy."

"Hey babe - well, well, well, you are all ready for bed early. I am shocked."

"Ariel, did you get dressed all by yourself?"

"Yep, I tried to wake you up, but you wouldn't get up, so I got myself dressed for bed," Ariel responded while lifting the pink ruffles on nightgown and twirling around.

"Oh, Ms. Trina, I'm—"

"No, baby. No need to apologize. You were tired and you got a nap. No biggie. And my baby is big enough to put her own nightgown on," Trina said while picking Ariel up and kissing her multiple times on her face. "But she's not old enough to take her bath all by herself," Trina giggled.

"Yes, I can mommy."

"No, Ms. Thang, You're not. Not yet so let's get this nightgown off and get you in the tub. Right after we take Twila home."

"No, it is okay; you don't have to do that. You can stay and give Ariel her bath, I can call my mom."

"You sure? I don't mind."

"Yes ma'am. My mom is probably only watching the news or something," Twila chuckled and shook her head. "My momma loves her some news. She can come and pick me up."

Trina laughed, "She sure does."

"Good Job Ariel! I'm proud of you!"

"Thank you," Ariel said shyly.

"*Thank you*," Twila mocked while hugging Ariel. Picking up her phone, she clicked mom and listened. The phone range four times and went to voicemail. "Hmmm, where is she?" Tapping her mom's contact again, she listened to the ringing before it yet again, move over to voicemail. "Maybe she fell asleep," she muttered.

"Everything ok?"

"Yeah, I think my mom went to sleep or something," she responded to Trina while pushing her mom's number again and again, voicemail answered.

"I can take you home; it's no—"

"Nah, it's okay. I can walk."

"You sure, it's getting dark out there," Trina frowned.

"It's all good. I walked home before. It's good exercise." Grabbing her book bag, she walked over to the door. "Bye Ariel, see you next time."

"Bye Twila!" Ariel giddily responded while jumping up and down.

"So much energy," Trina laughed

"Yes!" Twila agreed. "I will see you later Ms. Trina," she called out before walking out the door.

"Okay baby. Let me know when you get home."

"Okay," Twila called back into the house and headed on her way. Trotting down the front porch steps and glancing around at her surroundings, she grabbed her phone and tried calling her mother again. "Dang ma! What in the world are you doing?!" She mumbled as the voicemail did its thing again. "Oh well, I guess she went to sleep." *Finally finding news boring.* Chuckling, she waited for a car to pass before walking across the street. Two small children rode their bikes in her path.

"Excuse me," the little girl with big jumbo ponytails in her hair yelled out and whipped past Twila. Moving over, Twila looked down at her phone, a habit that she had. *Always looking down at that phone*, she heard her father's voice.

"Cuse' me," the boy version of the little girl who rode past called out, trying hard to catch up.

Stopping to allow the little boy room to pass, Twila looked through her phone, looking at nothing while two more children lagging behind, ran fast to catch up with the two other kids. Looking to see if any more kids were trailing behind, she began her walk home. A cool breeze filled the air as the sun was almost done setting.

"Hey! Give it back!" The little boy yelled before walking over to the front runner of the group.

"No! His opponent, the girl version of himself, yelled back and pushed the boy down to the ground.

"Ow! Stop!"

"Hey," Twila jogged over to the little boy and helped him up. "You ok?"

"Yeah."

Looking him over, Twila didn't see any signs of injury. "Be careful, okay."

"Okay," the boy said while dusting his pants off and getting back onto the bike. Twila looked at the girl who pushed him, but she was long on her way down the street. "Kids," she huffed while watching the boy ride slowly. A car horn caught Twila by surprise. Startled, she turned towards the blaring horn and saw the small blue car charging at her. Jumping out of the way, the car skipped the curb and quickly landed back onto the street, blowing the horn the entire time. "Oh my God, oh God, Oh my God!" Twila said over and over as she held her chest, horrifyingly watching the car until it was out of view.

CHAPTER 11

Who was that? And why did they try to run me down?

I know It wasn't Torri... she is out of jail. Torri gotta' be behind it somehow. Still feeling uneasy and nervous about the little blue car, Twila laid down on her bed and opened her nightstand drawer, pulling her diary out. Maybe they were drunk or something.

Really Twila! Her intuition roared at her. *They weren't drunk, I was the target.* Sighing, she grabbed her phone and punched Adriana's picture but quickly hit the end button. I'm sure she is still at her mom's house.

Hey girl, she typed in instead. You are not going to... No, no need to get Adriana all up into it, then she will be ready to go back and fight Torri all over again. I will find out who tried to run me down.

Hey... wyd...

In a matter of seconds, Adriana's response lit up the phone.

Nothing. Chillin.

You still at your mom's house...

Waiting on Adriana's response, Twila thought of the girls that were always hanging around with Torri. Who are they? She asked aloud. Why are they always with Torri? Like they have nothing else better to do.

Yeah. Ready to go home.

Twila chuckled at Adriana's reply. Still having trouble with her mom, I guess.

K. call me when you get some time.

K. as soon as my mother is done with this crazy bonding time.

Twila laughed and placed her phone on the nightstand. Sighing, she rolled over on her back, threw her diary over off to the side and closed her eyes. I'm glad those kids were out of the way and didn't get hit. Nothing but a bunch of lames around here. Speaking of lames... she said before Torri and her crew popped into her mind again. I'm so glad Adriana has come to her senses and stopped hanging around people like Torri and her gang. Crazy chicks. They deserve to... Twila's laptop stopped her mid-sentence. Not more homework, she said under her breath, sat up, and walked over to her desk. Probably another extra credit assignment. Opening her laptop, she began to feel hot. *"Slut"* leapt out at her. Followed by *"whore."*

Oh, that's what we doin' now?! She yelled and slammed her laptop shut. Torri entered her mind and she rolled her eyes. I know she ain't doing stuff like this now. I guess if she can steal and bully people at school, then she can certainly resort to internet bullying. It has to be Torri. Wait until I see her, I'ma- *ding*.

Looking over at her laptop, she quickly opened it and frowned. *"Slut"* popped out again, this time in bold purple letters. Looking at the sender's information, the number was from a 555 number.

"I can't even write nothing back!" She yelled and slammed her computer shut again. "Whoever it is don't even have the guts to use their number. A bunch of lames," she quipped and got up from her desk. Walking over to her bed, she turned back towards her desk and unplugged her laptop. Smacking her lips, she walked over to her window and looked out. A few boys were out throwing around a football while two women jogged by. Closing her curtain, she walked over to her beanbag and flopped down as she worked to calm her nerves. Her mind was still swirling, and her heart was still pounding at the cruel messages that she'd received. The fact that she couldn't reply back bugged her the most. Laying her head down, she thought about calling Adriana to vent about her almost untimely death, but she quickly ruled against it. That would only cause more problems.

"Damn it!" she said and readjusted herself. No matter how hard she tried, she couldn't get all the stuff that was happening out of her head. Listing them one by one, her mind went wild, consumed with all sorts of colorful thoughts which were all her new reality. "All the mess with Josh and his bouts with steroids, Torri and the bitch squad, Kyle..." she allowed her voice to level off.

Kyle... That was the biggest thing that took control of her mind. *Why didn't I call for help?* Twila slid out of her beanbag and onto the floor. All she could focus on now was Kyle's lifeless body lying cold on the slick rainy ground. *Only if I would've called for help, maybe Kyle would've lived, and Josh wouldn't be getting poked with needles full of poison.* Twila's mind took another turn and landed on Adriana. *If Adriana wasn't drinking that night, then Kyle would still be here.* Twila shook her head and tried to erase the last part of the memories from her mind. *No, that's not fair. Adriana got help for that and she's doing a lot better.*

"Hey baby. I guess I was tired," the bedroom door burst open with her mother full of energy, scaring Twila half to death. "Why didn't you wake me up when you got...Hey, you ok? You don't look right."

Twila shrugged her shoulders. "I'm ok, I guess. Just a lot on my mind." Josh and Kyle both danced around in her head, followed by the fact that someone had almost run her down, possibly causing her the same fate as Kyle and the messages on her computer sealed the deal with the negativity flowing around in her thoughts.

"A lot going on, huh?" Her mother said slowly and sat down on her bed.

"Yeah, just a lot going on with stuff at school."

"School? That's it?"

Twila hopped back onto her beanbag and grabbed a stuffed animal from her dresser. "Not just school," she said while looking over at her laptop. "All the stuff about Kyle. And then, mess with..." Twila stopped herself before she blurted about the small blue car. As far as her mother was concerned, all was well; there were no deranged people after her, ready to take her down. *No need to go into all the crazy stuff like that. It would only cause my ma to start trippin'.*

"Go ahead, I'm listening. Mess with what or who?"

"Nobody, I was just going to say mess with all the homework Ms. Engelman is throwing out at school. It's just too much."

"Uh huh. Okay. Well, when you're ready to talk and tell me the real reason, I'm here."

Twila nodded her head, stood up and stretched. "Yeah, ma." Twila leaned over and allowed her mother to kiss her on the cheek.

"How did you get home? I saw that you called me a few times."

"Ms. Trina drove me home," Twila answered quickly, thinking of the car that almost hit her and thankful that Trina wasn't busy giving Ariel her bath and was able to pick her up. *Me walking was a complete disaster.*

"Oh okay. I didn't even hear my phone. I'ma go back downstairs and see if I can catch that story I was watching earlier. I'm sure they will play it again before the night is over."

Twila collected her night gown and bath items. "Okay, I will be downstairs after I take my shower."

"Alright love," her mother said before walking out and closing the door. Shaking her head, Twila tried to shake away the negativity before going to take a long, exhilarating shower.

CHAPTER 12

I f you have not studied for the test, please do so! You only have two more weeks before we take the final exam and that is half your grade." Twila remained stoned faced while Ms. Engelman spoke about the importance of knowing all about pi and Pythagorean theory. *As if we would really need this stuff after graduation.*

"I need all of you on your A game when you're taking the test. I know I taught you, but you have to do your part too." Twila huffed internally as Ms. Engelman sat on her desk, giving the class a que that she was getting ready to give a lecture. "If you don't study at home, you—"

"Yes! As always, the bell caught her before she can get her rant going."

"Study and study hard! Don't wait until the last minute," Ms. Engelman rushed as kids poured out of the classroom. Why does she even do that! Twila blurted, joining Adriana as the two walked over to Twila's locker.

"'Cause she wants ya'll to be good at math! Math is so important in your day to day life Twila. Don't you get that?" Adriana mocked.

"Girl bye," Twila laughed while fumbling with her locker. "Ugh, I hate this thing! All this time and I still can't get my own locker open."

"Here, I got it."

"Nope, I will get it. I can't keep getting you to open my locker for me. I should be opening this thing!"

"Yeah, you really should."

Twila laughed and continued to fumble with her lock. "Finally!" She breathed as the lock popped open. "Told ya I will get it."

"Goooood job. You did it. I'm so proud of you."

"You real funny today," Twila laughed. "Okay."

Adriana giggled and opened her backpack, rummaging around in it. Twila glanced up, seeing Todd and James, two of Josh's fellow teammates, walk into the direction of the locker rooms. She gasped when she saw the Coach go behind them. I don't know where I put that gloss, Adriana said as she continued to search her contents. "No," Twila mumbled while thinking of what she saw the other day. Josh and his Coach, standing in the girls' locker room doing something that they had no business doing. *Well, they could have practice today.*

"Maybe I can borrow yours."

"Huh," Twila asked in a hushed whisper.

"Your gloss. Maybe I can borrow it."

"Um, yeah, sure."

"Aye! Hello?! Okay, I've been talking for the past two minutes and you haven't said a word. What is it? Did you see Josh sometimey butt and now your mind is all on him?"

"What, no. I ain't thinkin' bout that boy."

"Right. Oh shoot! The school is on fire!"

"It's all good."

"Um hmm! See! I knew you wasn't paying attention to a word I'm saying!"

"What? What are you talking about?" Twila muttered while keeping her eyes on the direction of the gym.

"I just told you that the school is on fire and all you said was "It's all good." I know the school is wack and all but dang, show a little compassion. At least act like you care."

"Girl, I know ain't nothing going on up in here," Twila chuckled.

"Uh huh, so, are you babysitting tonight?"

Twila looked over towards the entrance to the locker rooms. The looks on their faced troubled Twila; scared looks. Not the laughter and joking that they do while getting ready for practice.

"No, not tonight." Walking through the hallway, Twila gasped when she saw two more boys go into the locker room, the same looks etched across their faces. *I got to go in there. I need to see what's going on.* Looking at her phone, she sighed. *I will be late for the bus, but I have to see.*

"Let's go over to Crust tonight. Maybe we can catch—"

"Hey girl, can your dad drop me off home?"

"Yeah, he can do... what's going on? Was sup?"

Twila glanced at Adriana and then back at the locker room doors.

"What girl?!"

"Adriana, I saw something..." Twila stopped, Josh's threat filled voice interrupted her.

"You sawww... what?"

"What time is your dad coming?"

"In the next few minutes," Adriana answered while looking at her phone. "Was sup? You are acting like you've seen a ghos– uh oh, did you think you saw... *Kyle*?"

Twila stepped back to allow the cheerleaders room to walk by, her eyes following them. Gasping, her eyes grew wide when she noticed where they were going.

"Twila, what is wrong with—"

"Come on," Twila muttered and grabbed Ariana's shirt. "Come with me to the locker room real quick."

"Why, what's—"

"Just come on," Twila whispered. The girls walked quickly, following behind the cheerleaders, working diligently not to be noticed.

"Twi—"

"Shhh," Twila motioned. Waiting until the girls entered, she looked at Adriana and then walked to the entrance. Signaling for Adriana to join her, Twila opened the door and peeked inside. Adriana followed close behind as Twila walked in completely. Looking towards the office where she found the Coach, Josh… and the needle, she heard the cheerleaders burst out in laughter.

"Twila, what's in here besides the preppy—"

Twila put her hand up. "I will explain later." Moving closer to the office, careful not to get caught, she looked back at Adriana and then boldly walked to the office. To her surprise, the office was all clear. Except for Coach Snow's bull horn, "best Coach ever" coffee mug, and a mess of brown boxes.

CHAPTER 13

What is taking them so long? You would think they would already have the pizza ready. Always gotta' wait a long time just to get one pizza."

Twila shook her head and looked over at a group of kids who was laughing and having a good time. Looking back at Josh, she smiled, hoping to lighten his mood. Thoughts of him, his Coach, and the other teammates crossed her mind, but she quickly shooed it away. *Not going there tonight.*

"I wish they would shut up! What is so funny?!"

"Josh!"

"What?!"

Twila frowned at Josh, noticing the look of rage in his eyes. "What is the matter with you?!"

"Them! Over there wilin."

"So. They ain't messin' with us. Why you trippin'? There is something going on Josh and I need to know what it is."

"Nothing. I'm just ready to go."

"Already?! We just got here."

"Twila, I—"

"Here you go. Cheese only on one half and peperoni on the other."

"We can see that!" Josh blurted. "We know what we ordered!"

Twila frowned at Josh and then looked up at the waiter, feeling immensely embarrassed at Josh's behavior. "I'm sor—" The waiter stormed off before Twila could apologize on behalf of her boyfriend. Getting up from the table and rolling her eyes at Josh, Twila walked away and didn't look back.

"Girl, I told you before, you need to leave that boy alone. He is not good for you." Twila laid her head down on her beanbag as she listened to her Adriana give her the business about Josh. "You need to hit Byron up."

"Byron. Really, A? Byron? Byron with the braces? Girl bye."

"What?! He be askin' about you and he's cute."

Twila sat up and giggled. "Oh really, since when?"

"Uh, since forever but you are so into Josh that you don't see nobody else. Now that you are *finally* breaking up with that Josh, you can have some real—"

"Who said we were breaking up? I said Josh is acting crazy—"

"Like the jerk that he is."

Twila chuckled, "having some issues but I never said that I was going to break up with him. Twila stood up and stretched. He's just going through something, that's all. Everybody has bad days."

"Yeah but this is more than a bad day. This is more like a mental breakdown."

"Adriana, girl."

"Twila!"

"Hold on."

"Huh?"

"I forgot the salad dressing. Be back in a minute."

"Okay ma and can you get me some—"

"Sour gummy worms, I know."

Twila laughed, "I was going to say some apples, but the gummy worms will be so much better."

"Mmm hmm. Be back in a little while."

"Okay!" Twila closed the door and shook her head at Adriana.

"Um, you could've got your mom to get me something."

"Why didn't you ask? What do you want?"

"Nothing, I'm good. It's just the polite thing to do. You know, ask your best friend who is sitting right here if she wants something from the store."

"Alright!" Twila laughed aloud. "I got it! I will give you some of my gummy worms...or an apple."

"Girl bye! You know I don't want no apple. I want the good snacks."

"Apples are a good snack."

"You know what I mean."

Twila chuckled and walked over to her mini aquarium and peeked in. Grabbing the fish food, she sprinkled a few flakes inside and watched as the colorful school rushed to the top, working to win the battle of mealtime.

"Dang, Twila. Did you feed them things today? They are going crazy."

"They always go crazy when I put food in there."

"Speaking of crazy, what in the world was happening the other day?"

"Huh? Whatchu mean?" Twila replied while flopping down on her bed and grabbing her phone.

"The locker room... Preppy girls... all that. Was sup with that?"

"The *locker* room? What about—"

"Girl, stop. You know when you looked like you saw a ghost and the preppies was going into the locker room. You dragged me and—"

"Oh yeah."

"*Oh yeah*," Adriana mocked.

"It was nothing. Just thought I saw something." "Hey Maddie!" Twila smiled at her puppy as she entered the room, wagging her tail and slowly walked over to Adriana.

"Really Maddie? You always come to me first now you're going over to Adriana?"

"Yep, hey girl," Adriana smiled and sat on the floor next to Maddie. "Hell must've frozen over today, and nobody told me."

"Yeah, did it freeze over today? You not barking so it must've."

Twila burst out in laughter. "Shut up Adriana! My dog doesn't bark that much."

"Whateva! She's cute and all but she barks way too much. So back to the locker room. What—"

"Ugh! I told you it was nothing girl!"

"Twila Marie Ander"

"Oh no, nope! My momma is the only one who calls my whole government."

"Anyway," Adriana smacked lips and rolled her eyes. "Twila Marie Anderson. What is going on with you and the locker room stuff? You know *I know* it's more than just thinking you saw something? Was sup?"

Twila flipped over on her back, thoughts of Josh and his attitude crowded her mind, yet again.

Not a word, she heard him say. *Well, I won't tell anybody. Maybe I can just tell her and that's it.*

"Twila!"

"What! I am right here!"

"What is going on?"

"Nothing. I promise there is nothing going on. I just thought I saw someone, that's all."

"Uh huh, someone like who? Kyle?"

"Kyle? No... Kyle is no longer with us so that's impossible. Not Kyle... I just thought I saw someone who—"

"Okay, never mind. I guess you're going to keep it all to yourself and I will just have to find out by myself. No problem."

"Adriana, there is nothing—"

"Twila! Come and help me with the bags!"

Maddie's ears perked up at the sound of Twila's mother's voice. "And there she goes," Adriana laughed at Maddie as she leapt out of her lap, ran out of Twila's room and down the stairs.

"You know I will find out what you're hiding. You can't keep nothing from me."

"Yeah, I know. You're too nosey for that," Twila chuckled.

"And you know this."

Twila shook her head before walking out of her bedroom and down the stairs. Hey ma, what did you get?

"Just a few items. There are two bags left in the car."

"A'ight."

"Uh, don't stand there like you don't know what to do."

"Sorry, Ms. Sharon," Adriana giggled.

"Uh huh, you know better."

Adriana laughed and walked over to the door, Grabbing Maddie in the process. "You want to go outside? Huh? Come on, let's go outside."

"It's about time that you came out here," Twila quipped.

"It's just two bags, I thought you had it."

"Girl, you know when my mom says two, she means more like five or six." The girls laughed in unison, each grabbing a bag.

"Aye!"

Twila and Adriana both looked towards the sound of the voice, while Maddie began to do her usual, bark.

"Aye, Twila! Come here for a sec."

"Who's that?"

Twila squinted her eyes but couldn't make out the face. "I don't know."

"Who's that?!" Adriana yelled.

"Come here for a minute. I got to tell you something."

Following Adriana's lead, Twila called out. "Who's that?"

The girls both frowned as the figure moved closer, allowing them to see better.

"What is he doing here?" Adriana whispered. "And how does he know where you live?"

"James?"

"Yeah, let me talk to you real quick."

"About what?" Adriana questioned, not giving Twila time to respond.

"Yeah, about what?" Twila asked, although she had an inkling on what the surprise visit was all about.

"Whatchu want to talk to Twila about?"

James remained quiet, keeping his eyes fixed only on Twila. "Why you worried about it? You should be worrying about getting dem license back after you killed my boy."

In an instant, Adriana balled her fist up, put Maddie down on the grass, and trotted towards James.

"Adriana! Stop! Damn."

"I bet chu won't be talking all that smack when I hit yo butt wit' a car!"

"You the reason why..." James allowed his voice to trail off. Instead, he turned in the other direction, focusing his attention on the ice cream truck that was approaching.

"Adriana calm down!"

Twila put the bags back down in the trunk of the car and walked towards James.

"Adriana, take those bags and Maddie in the house for me. I got this. Let me see what he wants." Adriana shot James a devilish, raged filled glance before scooping Maddie up and walking in the house. Twila put her head down and then looked back up, trying to read James' face.

"What?"

"I wanted to talk to you about Coach." Twila froze. Although she knew in her gut why James decided to make a stop to her house, it was surreal hearing him actually say it.

"Coach," she played it cool. "Your coach?"

"Twila, I know you saw Josh and Coach in the girls' locker room."

"Josh and Coach... girls' lock—"

"A'ight, play dumb. Me and you both know that you saw what was going on. I was there and I saw you watching."

Twila was dumbfounded. She kept her mouth closed, waiting patiently for him to continue. "Coach is under a lot of pressure since your friend killed—"

Twila cut a sharp look at James, signaling him to watch his mouth.

"Before Kyle was kill... before the accident."

Twila softened her gaze and folded her arms. "Look James, I gotta' go. Just get to the point."

"Whateva you saw, just forget you saw it. That's all I wanted to say."

"Really, that's it? You came all the way over here just to tell me to *forget* what I saw or what you thought I saw."

"No, what I know you saw. We can get in a lot of trouble if it gets out that we are doing."

"What, Steroids?"

Immediately, Twila regretted saying that. She'd wished she'd continued to act as if she didn't know what was going on. Instead, her ego got the best of her.

"So, you did see."

"What else do you want James? I gotta' go."

"That's it. Keep your mouth shut Twila."

"Or what?" Again, Twila unintentionally allowed her ego to take over.

"Or I will tell everybody that you were actually the one driving the car the night Kyle was killed."

Twila gasped, not sure if she was hearing James, a boy whom she's known since elementary school, correctly.

"I don't want to do that but don't make me. You cool and all, but we can't let this get out. I'm sure your detective daddy and his boys won't want that all up at the police station." With that, James coolly strutted away from Twila, flagging the ice cream truck down as if nothing had happened.

CHAPTER 14

Laying down on her bed, Twila looked over at her buzzing phone. Josh's picture shined brightly on the screen, causing her to close her eyes and roll over on her side. Now, not only was Josh consistently on her mind, James added a whole extra layer of thoughts to hold her mind hostage. Vibrations vibrated her bed again. Josh stared at her with his signature smile, dimples and all. "What have you gotten yourself into Josh?" She whispered right before she hit the end button.

Knock, knock! "Hey baby. Whatcha doing?"

"Hey ma, just chillin'."

"Hmmm. Chillin' huh?"

"Yep, getting ready to do some studying."

"Studying, I see. So... how's everything going with Josh? Haven't seen him much and I haven't heard you talk about him lately."

Dang, again, already? She just asked about Josh the other day?! Twila drew a blank, not sure how to answer her mother and knowing full well that she had better not say what she as actually thinking. It was no doubt that she was trying to get information. Not just the "small talk, how you are doing" conversation she wanted her to believe.

"Josh? Josh is fine. He has a lot going on with football and everything. We went out and had pizza the other night."

"Oh okay."

Twila sat up on her bed and pulled her laptop off her nightstand, hoping that her mother would get the hint to leave.

"Alright, I will be downstairs. Call me when you're ready to talk about Josh." *Yesss, it worked*!

"Nothing is wrong, but okay," Twila giggled. As soon as her mother closed the door, Twila got to work, finishing what she had started days prior. *Steroids*, she typed in quickly. Just like before, the same information popped onto her screen.

Anabolic Steroids

Medical uses

Risk and side effects

"Yes," side effects, she mumbled and clicked on the link. *Kidney and liver disease* shot back at her like the words were a raging wildfire and she was surrounded by it all. "Oh no," she whispered. *Kidney and liver disease*, she repeated under her breath. Reading further, her eyes grew wider when she fingered across the article and saw that Steroids also causes changes in attitude. *Mood swings... irritability...depression...*and Suicidal tendencies, she read aloud. Oh no. No, no, no. *He's already mad all the time, I can't have him trying to kill himself.* Closing her laptop, she saw enough. I got to stop Josh from doing that. And James too, even though I don't like him right now, she quipped while placing her laptop down on the nightstand and getting up completely off her bed, determined to save Josh and his teammates from themselves and their Coach.

"You finally ready to see me?"

Twila stared at Josh for a few seconds before responding. "Not really, but I have something important I need to talk to you about."

"Oh-kay. Whatchu want to talk about?" Josh grabbed Twila's hand as they walked side by side in the neighborhood park, Maddie a few steps in front of them. Twila firmly gripped Maddie's leash as two joggers jogged by. To her and Josh's surprise, Maddie remained quiet.

"What, she ain't bark at them?" Josh chuckled.

"I know right, I can't believe she didn't," Twila muttered as she tried thinking of a way to bring the information about Steroids up without Josh becoming irritated.

"So, was sup?"

Twila scrambled internally to get her words together, careful not to come off too harshly. "Josh, I read some stuff about Steroids." Waiting to give Josh time to respond, she looked straight ahead and gave Josh's hand a comforting squeeze. "Josh?"

"I told you to stay out of it."

"I know what you said but I can't just stay out of it. I care too much about you Josh."

"Twila, you don't know what's really going on. I don't want you—"

"Yeah but I know that you or nobody else should be taking steroids and your *coach* definitely shouldn't be injecting you with—"

Josh grabbed Twila by the shoulders. "I told you to not worry about that!" Smacking his hands off her shoulders, Twila pushed Josh.

"Don't you ever grab me like that again."

An older man looked over at Twila and Josh with a concern look etched across his face, Maddie began to growl.

"It's ok girl," Twila comforted her puppy.

"I-I'm sorry," Josh stammered. "You know I would never hurt you, right?"

Twila bent down to pet Maddie. "Yeah, I know," she said slowly.

"I just got a lot going on. The Coach—"

"The Coach what Josh? What about the Coach?"

Josh sighed and sat down on top of a picnic table. Twila walked over slowly and sat down on the attached seat, picking Maddie up and rubbing her paws.

"Ever since Kyle died, he's been trippin'."

Twila remained quiet, giving Josh a respectful pause.

"Coach just wants to win. Kyle was who made our team the best team in the state. We kept losing so—"

"Your coach started giving y'all steroids so—"

"We can win again. We can be the best team... even without Kyle."

"Josh! That's crazy and..." Twila stopped and put her head down, working to calm her nerves so that Josh would continue to trust her. "Sorry," she said softly.

"We only have to do it during the season. Josh paused for a second before he continued. "Well, that's how it started. Then Coach said that it works best if we just do it all year long. It's for the best, you know." Josh looked out in the distance before continuing. "Maybe I can get a scholarship so I can go to TPU."

"Josh, that stuff is dangerous," Twila said while gently putting Maddie down on the ground. There are other schools you can go to. Townsend is not the only school."

"Yeah but it's the best college and a lot of boys make it to the NFL there. I want to do better for myself than my dad did. I want to make sure my mom and Ariel are straight. So, I just need to do what Coach—"

"I feel you Josh but—"

"But what?!"

Twila turned her head and stood up. "I will call you later."

"Twila, I didn't mean—"

"Yeah, I know. You didn't mean what you said, and you would never hurt me. I got it." Flashing a fake smile, Twila walked away, Maddie quickly walking beside her.

CHAPTER 15

Walking into Harriet High was like walking into a prison. Kids walked through the halls as loudly as usual but in Twila's mind, they were a bunch of kids, holding the big bad secret that the football Coach was forcing his team to inject steroids.

"Hey girl! I've been calling you."

"Hey Adriana."

"What's wrong wit' you?"

Twila wanted to blurt it out; just say it. *The football Coach is making the team take steroids*! *A drug that will and can kill them*! "Nothing, she mumbled instead."

"Okay, I was calling to tell you that I got a new job. Start tomorrow."

"Dat's was sup!" Twila said, trying to sound enthused.

"I know right! I need all the money I can get, and I can finally get my parents off my back about staying *busy*." "*No relapses*," Adriana mocked her mother. "Then my dad comes right behind her and says, having nothing to do is dangerous. You need to get a job."

Twila chuckled, "yeah."

"Twila, girl, are you sure everything is ok?"

"Yeah, I'm good. Just..." Twila stopped midsentence as James walked by, looking at her as if she was the devil.

"Ugh, what is wrong wit' that boy!" Adriana called out and rolled her eyes. "What did he want the other day?"

"It was nothing. Just had a question about Josh."

"Josh? Don't he talk to Josh every day? Why is he asking you about—"

"Girl just forget it!" Twila snapped. "Let's go and get this day over with. I need to be at the football field before anybody else gets there."

"The field? Why? The first game isn't until Sep—"

"Because I'm going to their practice today."

"Practice? What's going on at practice? You never been to practice before, why now? Wait, does this have anything to do with the preppies, the locker room, and James coming over—"

"Nope, just decided I need to support my man more than I am supporting him. That's all. I got a test today so I gotta' go. Meet me at my locker right after school. Can your dad give me a ride today?"

"Uh, yeah. I will text him to let him know."

"A'ight, see you later." Twila walked away quickly and headed to her class, eager to get the day done as fast as time permitted.

"Come on! Let's go! Ingram! You not moving fast enough! Let's go!"

Twila shook her head as the Coach yelled and taunted the football players. "Harriet High's finest. Humph, yeah right."

"Hey girl. I had to stop by Ms. Duncan's room and get the stupid extra credit work that my mom is making me do. Was sup?"

"Hey chick, just watching Josh kill himself."

"What?" Adriana laughed. "They always practice and play like that in practice."

That ain't what I'm talking about. Steroids and all the information about them burned into Twila's mind. "Yeah, but it's like their Coach is pushing them way too hard."

"Well, they are the best in the state. I guess that's why they have to work so hard."

"Nope, that ain't why."

"Okay, then what is it?"

Twila put her head down, debating whether or not she should tell Adriana about the football team's secret. Looking at her friend, her friend since elementary school, she decided to go forward. "A, if I tell you something, you got to promise that you will keep it between me and you. Nobody can know about it."

"Yeah, you know you can trust me. Was sup?"

Twila sighed, not sure if she was making the right decision to trust Adriana. "James likes you," she blurted out instead, quickly losing her nerve. Twila stared at Adriana, knowing that she was getting ready to get roasted on for such a lame comment.

"Really, Twila. That's the big secret? Really?" Adriana laughed. "You got to come better than that. Was sup?"

"White! If you miss one more time, you are out!"

Twila rolled her eyes at the Coach. "Jerk," she quipped.

"Okay, what is going on with you and the Coach? You never had a problem with him before. What did he do to you?"

Twila grabbed her phone and looked at the time. "What time is your dad coming?"

"Whenever I call him. Why?"

"Okay, so we have some time then. Come on, let's go to the locker room real quick."

"No, Twila, what is going on? I am tired of going to the locker room. What is it about the locker room all of a sudden? It is– Wait, is it something about Coach Snow? Coach Snow is really a man! I got it!"

"Coach snow... girl no," Twila giggled. "This has nothing to do with Coach Snow."

"Okay, something is up. What is it?"

"I just need to go and see something. Come on before they get finished."

"I saw your girl the other day."

Josh sat still on the sidelines, watching his teammates practice. "Okay," he replied dryly.

"You do know that she knows about the shots, right?"

Josh looked over at James and nodded his head. "Yeah, but she ain't goin' say nothing. We good."

Both boys perked up as two of their teammates got into a shoving match. "Aye! Boyd, get over there on the bench!' Coach Davis yelled. "You're out for today!"

"Yeah, I told her that she better not say nothing or—"

"Or what?" Josh sat up. "Whatchu mean you told her not to say nothing. Did you threaten my girl?"

"Threaten her? Nah man, it wasn't nothing like that. I just told her that if she said anything, we would all be in trouble. Not just us, but the whole school."

Josh stared at James for a few seconds. "Yeah," he squirmed in his seat. "We got to do this, just for this year and then when we get to college, it will all be over."

"Yup," James agreed. "I got to get the scholarship this year. My family ain't got the money for me to go to college so I got to do what I got to do."

"I feel you. My mom is counting on a scholarship. I got to get in so I can help her and my sister. Live a better life. I'm tired of seeing my mom struggle."

"I know Whatchu mean. Just got to—"

"Was sup y'all."

"What up," Josh and James said in unison.

"Coach trippin' today. Kicked me out for no reason," Anthony said while pouring bottled water on his face.

"Coach always trippin'" Josh replied.

"Yeah, he been acting like that ever since Kyle passed," James added.

The boys looked out into the field, watching their teammates fumble and make all kinds of small mistakes. Well, in Coach Davis' eyes, mistakes that will cost everybody everything.

"I'll holla at y'all later." I'ma go in the front and wait for my girl.

"Yo, you know you can't leave," Josh said.

Why, was sup? Coach already threw me out of practice and I ain't goin' keep sitting here with y'all."

"Injection day man," James joined in.

"Nah, I already had mine. I'm good for right now."

Josh and James watched Anthony until he was out of view. "Why he actin' like it don't matter?" Josh asked while shaking his head.

"I don't know. I guess he just looking at it like he got to do what he got to do," James replied.

"Yeah, I guess." Josh said and put his head down. Thoughts of Twila filled his mind; thoughts of her speaking on the dangerous, and in some cases, deadly side effects from taking steroids. *Man, what did I do?*

"Twila, will you hurry up? Somebody is going to come in here in a minute," Adriana hissed.

"In a sec girl," Twila responded while rummaging through the Coach's belongings, working to find some hard evidence of his crime. "Nothing," she smacked her lips and placed his bag back in its rightful position, careful not to move anything out of place on the desk.

"What in the hell are you up to and why are we in this stinky ole boy's locker room? I thought we were going to the girls'?"

"Who said we was going to the girls'?"

"Um, maybe because you've been focused on the girls' locker room for the past week. Or maybe because we are not supposed to be in here! Pick one."

Twila gave Adriana a harsh side-eye. "I'm trying to find something."

"Yep, you mentioned that. Now tell me what it is?!"

"Proof."

"Proof of what? Twila you are really—"

"Steroids, Twila huffed. Okay? I am looking for something that will prove that the Coach is into steroids."

"Steroids?"

"Yeah," Twila sighed. "I found out about it a few days ago. Adriana, you got to promise me that you won't say anything. I told Josh that—"

"Josh? Josh knows about his Coach using steroids."

Twila briefly looked upwards, "Josh is the one getting the steroids."

Adriana gasped, grabbing Twila's attention.

"His Coach has been injecting him with it...and James."

"What?!"

"Yeah, that's why you got to promise me that you won't say anything."

Adriana leaned against the cold, hard wall. "So that's why James came to your house the other day. It was about the steroids."

"Yep. Let's talk about it after we get out of here. I will come back again and look one day soon. He got to have evidence somewhere."

"Why are you looking for evidence? I thought you said that I can't tell anybody, so I am guessing that means you're not planning on telling anybody either... right?"

"Nope, keeping my mouth shut. Just want it."

"O-kay. For what?"

"Uh, just because. Being the daughter of a detective kind of gets the best of me," Twila replied while heading towards the exit.

CHAPTER 16

hy don't you try the coconut this time? It's really good."

"No thanks," Twila smiled at her dad before biting a big chunk of her Popsicle. I will stick with grape.

"Yeah, good ole grape. Do you want to take a bite of mine? Don't sleep on the coconut."

"Oh my gosh! You too?"

"What?"

"Don't sleep? You sound like ma."

"What? Your mom and I are cool. Wait, not cool...lit."

"Ugh! Y'all need to stop! Both of you," Twila and her dad both laughed and continued their weekly walk through Arbor Springs infamous harbor. One of the best times of the week for Twila; quality time with her dad. She always found a way to release all her cares and just focus on what her dad called, the date with her old man, but Twila's mind would not play along. Instead, thoughts of steroids and the dangers of using them took over like a raging tsunami.

"So dumplin', how's everything going? How's school?"

Twila took another bite of her Popsicle, hoping that would soothe her thoughts. "School's... School's good," she answered. Looking at the water, she admired how the water always perfectly caught the decorated lights that lined the park just right. "I have a test coming up that I'm a little nervous about."

"You, nervous? I can't believe that. You are so good with school."

Twila took a quick lick of her Popsicle, thinking of not the school or test but the shenanigans going on within her school. "Yeah, I'm usually ok, it's just this test is going to be pretty hard."

"Well, dumplin', it's like that sometimes. Just have to study harder."

"Yeah," Twila quickly agreed. James and most importantly, Josh held her attention, but it was no way she could tell her father; the big, bad, and bold detective that would surely take care of the entire situation. *What about their health? They could die.*

"Are you ready for some skating next weekend? Candice has been talking about it all week. I'm so glad you two are getting along dumplin'. It means the world to me that my two favorite girls are cool with each other."

"Yep," Twila responded and licked more of her Popsicle.

"Yep... that's it?"

"Yeah," Twila chuckled. "I mean, what else am I supposed to say dad?"

"Well, I guess I should be grateful that that's all you said."

"How about a boat ride? It's a nice night."

"Okay, sounds good to—"

The rush of sirens stopped Twila midsentence.

"What is going on now?" Fredrick asked as he looked around, noticing hushed whispers coming from all directions.

"Clear the walkway!" A police officer called out as two paramedics quickly ran past Twila and her dad.

"He just fell out!" a spectator said loudly as she walked by with a group.

"Somebody said he was drunk!" Another yelled.

"Hmm, that solves it, Fredrick. Somebody had too much to drink," Twila's dad said as he continued to look around.

"Well, it is Friday," Twila commented. "Maybe the person was down here at a party or something."

"Yeah, maybe."

"Is he breathing?" A girl in the budding crowd asked.

"I don't know. They are taking him to the hospital now," answered a fellow onlooker. "I think so. I heard the police say he was drunk."

"Come on Dumplin', we can take that boat ride another time. Let's go home."

Twila threw her Popsicle wrapper in the garbage and followed quickly behind her father to his car.

"Take your pick, I have all types you can try!"

"No thanks. I have my own," Twila said quickly, not ready to put her lips on her stepmother's lip gloss. *I don't know where her lips been.*

"Okay, if you change your mind, they are all over there on my makeup counter. Have any one of them you want."

"Okay," Twila responded. *I promise, I won't be changing my mind. Why do I feel like I am talking to my older sister and not my stepmother? This lady is way too young for my daddy.*

That girl just got out of high school. Fred ought to be ashamed of himself, Twila heard her mother's voice. Chuckling, she sat down at Candice's make up table and smiled, trying to lighten the mood. "What's this?" She asked as she picked up a blending sponge. Although she already knew what it was, she asked anyway, so that her dad would be proud that his *girls* were getting along and to make Candice feel as if she could actually teach something.

"That's what you call a beat brush! Blends your makeup together and makes it flawless. Want to try?"

"Uh, no thanks, I was just wondering."

Authorities say the teenager nearly drowned tonight in Arbor Springs.

Twila looked towards the door and stood up, hoping to hear better. Walking out of her father's room, she stood in the hallway and listened. Her father sat on the couch in front of the TV and watched the news report...

"That's right, Emily. Police aren't releasing the victim's name as of yet, but they are saying that it was a close call tonight as paramedics worked for hours to stabilize the teen who nearly lost his life at the Arbor Springs Harbor just a few hours ago. We are told that alcohol may be a contributing factor. More details will be available soon. This is Amber

Martinez reporting live for Action News District Eight."

Walking down the stairs, Twila looked over at Maddie's cage and then at her father.

"So, the kid almost drowned," Fredrick said and shook his head. "I hope the poor kid will be alright."

"Yeah," Twila said as she grabbed her phone off the charger and pushed Adriana's number.

Hey, did you hear about a boy almost drowning? She typed into her phone.

"Dumplin'... you've never drank before, right?"

Twila chuckled, "No daddy and where is this coming from?" she laughed. "When have you known me to want to drink?"

"Just askin'. I'm sure the kid who nearly drowned parents don't know that he may have been drunk. Thought I'd ask."

"Nah, dad, never had a drink before and don't plan on it."

"Good, baby. That's good. Drinking is no good. You know what happened when—"

"I got it dad, when Adriana had her problem with drinking. I got it."

"Okay, just making sure."

Yep, I just saw it on the news. Adriana's response flashed onto Twila's screen.

I wonder who it was...

Putting her phone down on the chair, Twila picked up her book off the coffee table and sat Indian style next to it.

Hey baby. Just checking on you.

Twila smiled and typed in a response to her mother.

Hey ma, I'm good.

They said teen... so most def somebody from school.

Yeah, Twila replied quickly to Adriana.

Call me in the morning. Love you.

K. Twila typed into her phone, following it up with a few heart emoji's. Closing her mother's text, she turned to Adriana's.

Yeah, prob so. Want to go to the mall tm...

What? Twila laughed at her father while he shook his head.

"Nothing. You and that phone. I wonder what would happen if you didn't have a phone."

"I don't know, and you and mom will make sure I don't have to find out, right?" Twila answered with a laugh.

"Hmmm," her dad responded before walking out of the living room.

Yep... I'm off

K... tm...10

K, I will meet you there. Ttyl

Bye

Twila threw her phone on the chair beside her and laid her head down. Thinking of Josh, she quickly grabbed her phone and then changed her mind. Never mind... He probably won't answer anyway, she quipped and laid back down on the chair.

"Hey girl, why are you just sittin' here? You ok?"

Twila rolled her eyes and smiled her brightest fake smile. "I'm good Candice. Just chillin'."

"Oh okay. Let me know if you need anything."

For my dad to find another wife. "K," she blurted out instead. *That was mean, I need to leave that chick alone.* Waiting for Candice to walk out of the living room, she smacked her lips lightly and looked over at her phone. Josh's face displayed causing her to feel mad and happy all at the same time. *Should I answer?* Continuing to keep her eyes on her phone, she sighed. *I guess so.*

"Hello," she answered nonchalantly.

"Yo, did you hear?"

Sitting up, Twila frowned at the urgency in Josh's voice. "Hear bout' what?"

"Did you hear what happened to James?"

"James? No what happened to... oh no, not the drowning thing."

"Yeah, he fainted and now he's at the hospital."

Twila wasn't sure if she should tell Josh that she was actually at the harbor when it happened or tell him that she'd heard on the news. *If I tell him I was there when it happened, he would probably think that I'm keeping stuff away from him; it would be the whole Adriana secret and the drinking thing all over again. The latter is best.* "Uh, yeah, I heard it on the news, but they didn't say that it was James. How do you know it was—"

"'Cause, his pops called Coach and Coach called all of us."

"Oh... well, is he going to be ok?" A few seconds of silence passed. "Josh?"

"Uh, yeah... Well, they hope so. He hasn't woken up yet."

"Aw man." Twila looked over at her sleeping puppy and repositioned herself on the couch. "I hope he will be ok. The news said something about him possibly drinking. Do you think—"

"Nah, James don't drink; he hates alcohol. So that's not it."

"Oh, the news said..." Twila voiced trailed off and completely stopped as her mind took completely over. Steroids leapt into her thoughts, followed by all the terrible side effects that can come with taking them. *Oh no...Please don't let it be because of the steroids... Oh no...*

"Twila?"

Steroids... Steroids...Steroids.... Drugs... those words contained her mind; not allowing anything else in.

"Yo! Twila?"

"Uh yeah. What?"

"Was sup, you blanked out on me. Was sup?"

"Uh, nothing. Hey. I'ma call you back."

"Call me back? Why?"

"Um, I just need to call my mom real quick. It's getting late and you know how my mom is when I'm staying with my dad. Gotta' call her before it gets too late."

"A'ight but don't go runnin' your mouth."

"Whatchu mean?" Twila said in a voice above a whisper.

"Nah, I just know how you like to go searching for stuff. Just don't be going around talking about it and definitely don't talk about it with your pops."

"No, no, I wasn't planning on saying anything," Twila lied. "I just need to call my mom. I'll call you back in a few minutes."

Josh sighed. "A'ight then."

"K," Twila said and clicked her phone off and immediately opened her search button. *Steriods*, she typed in too fast, spelling it incorrectly. Hitting the autocorrect, *Steroids* popped into her search bar and with that, all of the side effects lined directly under it. She gasped when she saw fainting. *Fainting is caused by a drop in blood pressure called Vasovagal reaction,* she read quietly. Oh no, you can faint from using them.

"Whatchu doing dumplin'? Working on some homework?"

Quickly closing her search on her phone, Twila looked up at her father. "Yep, yes daddy, doing some research. Got a paper due in a few weeks and thought I'd get started."

"That's my baby, always studying."

Twila gave a half smile, her eyes following her father until he was halfway up the stairs.

Oh no... no... If James is in the hospital from using Steroids, then it is all his Coach's fault. Twila put her head down, realizing just how real the situation had become.

CHAPTER 17

The hotdogs are almost ready! Come and get you one."

Twila followed behind her uncle John, her father's one and only brother and stood next to the grill, looking around at all of her family from her father's side, watching them all try to mingle and get along with Candice's family. Twila laughed at her aunt, Bunny, as she gave one of Candice's sisters a mean stank eye. *Really Aunt Bunny*, Twila giggled.

"Chile look at Bunny," another one of Twila's aunts, Sharla said to her sister Debbie and shook her head. "She gon' wind up smacking that girl before the day is over. Watch what I tell y'all. I don't know why Fred got us all up in here with them people. He knows we all don't like each other."

Twila laughed and shook her head as her Aunts Sharla and Debbie went on and on with their usual gossip.

"Yeah, I don't even know why Freddie married that little young girl," Debbie replied. "He should've stayed with Sharon."

"Y'all stop all that gossiping and try to have a good time," Brenda, Twila's father youngest sister intervened. "Freddie married her so now she is our sister."

"Naw she ain't," Aunt Bunny said loudly. "That girl ain't no sister of ours!"

"Twila, baby, go and get me a bottled water. My knee is about to break wide open. This arthritis chile."

"Okay, Aunt Sharla. *They are always talking about somebody*. Walking over to the cooler, she grabbed a bottled water for her aunt and a juice pack for herself.

"I heard the boy was on drugs."

Twila stopped in her tracks.

"Yeah, they said something on the news about it possibly being due to alcohol, but I don't believe that. That boy was on something else. Maybe he had a drink but that wasn't all he had."

Twila pretended that she was looking for another type of drink in the cooler as she focused on the conversation two of her grandmother's friends from church were having.

"Girl, these kids today get into all types of mess."

"Hey Dumplin'; you having a good time?"

Quickly turning around, she smiled at her father. "Uh yes daddy."

"Good, Everything ok? You look pale. You sure you feeling ok?"

"Yes, just getting a little hot out here, that's all." *Literally*, she quipped quietly.

"Okay, why don't you go on in the house for a while? Cool off for a bit. I can bring you a plate if you want me to."

"Oh no, I'm good dad."

"Sharon! Hey girl. Glad you could make it."

"Hey Deb, Hey Bunny. Y'all done giving y'all sister-in-law a hard time? I know y'all over here acting up."

"Humph, that girl ain't no sister-in-law of mine. You my sister-in-law," Bunny replied while fanning herself with a small envelope.

"Chill out Bunny."

"Oh Fred, I'm just messin'."

"Well, my wife can hear you so stop messin'."

"Sharon, thanks for coming," Fredrick said and gave his ex-wife a quick peck on the cheek.

"Hmm mmm," Sharon mumbled.

Twila enjoyed the exchange between her parents; it was no secret that she wanted them to get back together. Or for her father to at least marry someone closer to his age and not Candice's.

"How are you Sharon?" Candice spoke and stood next to her husband.

"Candice," Sharon responded and turned towards Twila and smiled.

"Twila! You know better than to just be standing over there and not say anything to your mother."

"Hey mommy. I was coming over."

"Hmm mmm, you better." Twila hugged her mother and took a gulp of her juice pack. "You get something to eat yet? I'm not staying here all day so as soon as you eat, we are out of here."

"No, not really hungry ma. I'm going to go give Aunt Sharla her water and then I will grab a hamburger, just to say I got something."

"Alright baby. At least the little woman isn't cooking it. You will eat something real over here for a change."

"Ma..."

"Alright... okay."

Twila laughed as she proceeded to walk over to her aunt.

"Chile! That little boy died!"

Twila frowned and looked towards the voice. Candice's aunt had a look of horror all over her face. "The boy who they found at the harbor has died!" Twila felt as if her knees were going to go out and she would fall, right there in front of everybody.

"Whats" and "oh nos" filled her father's backyard.

"Hey Dumplin'. I just got a text from my partner; I need to go to the station for a while. Eat as much as you like, and I will stop by your mom's later."

"Uh, um, okay," Twila managed to speak.

"You sure you alright? You look so pale to me. Why don't you go in the house and lay down for a while before you and your mom take off?"

"Fred, what's wrong?"

"I'll be back Candice. I got to get to the station to start an investigation. Got to do a preliminary investigation on the kid who died."

"Uh," Twila let out a faint cry.

"What's wrong Twila?" Candice asked followed by her mother.

"Baby, are you ok?"

"Yeah ma, I'm good. Just hot." James' face filled her thoughts as her family gathered around, looking for information from her father to fuel the neighborhood and church gossip.

Action News District Eight Special Report...

The Arbor Springs community is mourning the loss of one of their own tonight. Harriet High's senior, James Speight, has died.

185

The family decided to take him off life support one week after he was found unconscious at the Arbor Springs harbor. Doctors say a large amount of Anabolic- androgenic steroids were found in his system along with toxic amounts of opioids. The Arbor Springs Police Department has decided to look into the matter. More on this story as it develops.

"Wow that is so sad. Did you know him Twila?"

Twila looked over at her mother with tears in her eyes. "Yep, he played football with Josh." Springing up from the couch, Twila ran up the stairs to her bedroom.

CHAPTER 18

Settle down students! We are ready to get this assembly started! Let's go and get settled down!"

Twila sat down on the bleachers next to Josh and Adriana. "I wish she would go ahead and start this assembly already so we can go back to class and get this day over with!"

"I know right! I'm tired already and we just got here."

"Y'all both be quiet and just wait until the lady gets started."

Twila looked at Josh and rubbed his back. "I guess you're having a bad day. I mean James was your friend and all."

"Yeah, but that doesn't give him the right to act crazy towards us."

"Adriana."

"What? He should know better not to act that way towards me. I would say you, but you tolerate it so..."

Twila turned her attention away from Adriana and back on Josh. "You ok?"

"Yeah, I'm good. Just got a lot on my mind."

Twila continued to rub Josh's back as she surveyed the auditorium. Mounds of kids poured in, mostly glad that the day was started with a free pass out of class; most of them not caring about the real reason why they were all pulled out of first period so early in the morning.

"Good Morning Harriet High!"

The kids continued to chatter amongst themselves as the principal spoke up on the podium.

"I said, Good Morning Harriet High!" She yelled louder.

A few *good mornings* rumbled through the crowd.

"I would like to start by saying Harriet High is a school full of strength and courage."

The chatter began to quiet down as teachers sent warning looks and hand gestures to their students.

"It is a time of mourning here at our school as we lost a student last night. James Speights was one of our rising stars; one of our football stars."

The school was in full listening mode now, waiting on their principal to continue with her statements. "If any of you need anything during this difficult time, please do not hesitate to let me or any of the staff know. Please feel free to talk with your teachers if you are unconfutable talking with the office staff. We are all family here at Harriet High and we are all here to help. Please remember that as you go on with your day." Ms. Hanks paused briefly before she continued. "I want you all to understand that you are loved here! We are all here to support each other so if you are feeling down or have questions about anything, we have counselors that will be here all week. So, you have me, any of the staff in the office, your teachers, and counselors to help you through this. Have a wonderful day and remember that you are loved!"

Twila shook her head as Adriana rolled her eyes and stood up, trying to be one of the first ones out of the auditorium before it got too crowded to see a way through. "Come on before it gets crazy," she yelled back behind her, halfway down the bleachers.

Twila grabbed Josh's hand but Josh pulled away. "What's wrong?"

"You go ahead. I got to stay behind and talk to the Coach about something. I will see you later."

"Josh, no, not that again."

"Oh nah, nothing like that, I just need to ask him something, that's all. I will see you later today."

Twila stood in her section and watched Josh as he walked quickly down the bleachers and towards his coach's office.

"Again," Twila muttered as she stepped onto the sidewalk near the church. *First Kyle and now James, both from our football team.* Twila surveyed her surroundings. People from all over were there to pay their final respects to James. A boy who was now remembered as one of the best who picked up a football in her town. That was everyone's label once they died and played any type of a sport. They could be benched half of the time and still, once they pass, they would get the label as one of the best around.

"Hey girl," Adriana spoke dryly. "I do not want to be here right now."

"Yeah," Twila agreed and hugged Adriana.

"Well, at least I didn't *kill* James. I don't have to feel all guilty this time."

"Adriana, stop it. We all know what happened to Kyle was an accident. We all moved on from that."

"Yeah, I guess," Adriana said. "Look," she pointed at a group of boys walking towards them, all with solemn looks planted on their faces.

Twila frowned at the person, in her eyes, was responsible for all of this, Coach Davis. She watched as he shook hands with James' father and brother. The football team followed their Coach's lead, all shaking the family's hands. A slow, steady rain began to fall as people piled up in a line, ready to go into the church.

"Why?!" A harsh sob from the crowd echoed, causing everyone to turn. "Why James?! Nooo!"

Twila put her head down as a distraught teen holding a toddler walked by.

"Sup y'all," Josh walked up and quickly hugged Twila. "I see his baby momma taking things hard. Too bad she gave that man a hard time when he was alive."

"Say word!" Adriana cut in. "James had a baby?"

"Yep," Josh answered and looked around the crowd. "He had two."

Twila looked at Josh like he had lost his mind. "Two babies?"

"Yeah, I don't see the other baby momma though. Maybe she's with the family since her and James was together and all."

Twila's mind went into overdrive. *Two kids will grow up without their dad because of drugs. Harriet High's football Coach is the cause of two kids growing up without a father.* Looking over at Coach Davis, Twila smacked her lips. *I should tell daddy who's responsible for James' death.*

"Y'all ready to go in? The family wants everybody from school to sit together."

"Yeah, okay," Twila answered but kept her eyes on the Coach as he walked by, nodded his head, and walked into the church. "Ugh," she mumbled. Walking behind Josh and beside Adriana, Twila's eyes moved through the crowd already seated. Some were in tears, some were engaged in hushed conversations, but all had the ugly look of somber on their faces, causing Twila to produce a single tear in her right eye. Looking up in the front, she turned her head as James' body laid still in the open casket.

"Y'all want to go up there?"

Twila looked at Josh and grabbed his hand. "If you want to," she answered in a whispered voice. Twila gave an empathetic look to a pair that was reading the obituary.

"You coming Adriana?" Josh asked and held out his hand.

"No, I'm good; y'all go. I will hold our seats."

Twila looked at Adriana, pleading with her to join them but she knew that was a zero to none chance that she would; all that she went through during Kyle's services. Although she was locked away, she still felt the effects. Twila inhaled quietly and walked closely with Josh. With each step, she felt as if her feet were as heavy as bricks and her stomach was as light as a feather. The guilt consumed her, and the word *Steroids* took its rightful place in her mind. *I need to tell.* Squeezing Josh's hand, she felt that he too was extremely tensed. Although, he did everything in his power not to show it. *No, I can't. What about Josh and the rest of the team?* Looking down at the baby boy version of James, Twila let out a small cry. *I got to, for his kids' sake.* Finally reaching the casket, Twila looked away and then back at James. She rubbed Josh's back as he held his head down, working overtime to keep her feelings, her guilt intact about the fact that she knew all about the school's secret and kept it all to herself. *I should've said something. Then if I do say something, our school would be in a lot of trouble. I can't.* Twila's mind was like a roller coaster at an amusement park, right at the part where it was getting ready to take the passengers down from the highest level. Her mind went around and around. Up and down as she stood in front of James' lifeless corpse.

"How are you guys holding up?"

Twila looked over to see Coach Davis standing next to Josh as if he didn't have a care in the world.

"Okay, I guess," Josh answered.

Twila kept her mouth shut and eyes away from the Coach.

A long pause took over while more people filled the church. Twila, Josh, and the Coach all stepped aside to allow an elderly couple time to quickly view James before his funeral started.

"He's so young," the woman cried.

"Yeah, gone too soon," the man said and hugged the woman, both of them walking away slowly.

"Hey, Josh. We are having a quick meeting today after the services. Make sure you make plans to come by. Only be about five, ten minutes. The most, twenty. Just want to go over some stuff."

Josh looked at Twila and then back at his Coach. "A'ight. I will be the—"

"Um, Josh. I think it's best that we go over and see James' family after the services. Don't you think so?"

"Josh, it will only take a minute," Coach Davis said while looking at Twila.

Twila rolled her eyes and looked over towards the entrance. Coach Snow and a few of the girls from the track team walked in. Twila looked at Adriana and Adriana shrugged her shoulders. *Well, I guess Coach Snow wants to pay her respects too. I wonder does she know about Coach Davis and what he's been up to with his football team.*

"Excuse me. The family has arrived," a man dressed in all black, called into the microphone. "We're asking that everyone please take their seats."

"Come on Josh." Grateful for the interruption, Twila slightly pulled Josh away from his Coach and proceeded to their seat.

"Girl, y'all sure stayed up there a long time. What in the world?" Adriana whispered.

"Josh and his so-called Coach were talking. He wants the team to—"

"Shhh, here comes the family," Josh interrupted.

"Everyone, please stand," the same man who informed the crowd that the family had arrived, said into the microphone. Twila looked around as guest began to stand, showing James' family the utmost respect. James' parents walked in first, his mother held an infant girl, most assumingly had to be James' other child because she was the splitting image of James and the little boy who came in tow with his distraught mother moments prior. Twila held back tears as she watched James' mother cry. Looking over at the coach, she rolled her eyes and moved them to look straight ahead. *Standing there like he has nothing at all to do with why James is up there in that casket.* Twila closed her eyes and prayed that the service would move quickly. The more time she spent at the funeral, the more guilty she'd become.

CHAPTER 20

"Two deaths and you knew both of the boys huh?"

Twila looked over at her grandmother and nodded her head. "Yes grandma, I knew them both."

"Sharon, we might have to take this girl to the altar Sunday. Why so many people dying 'round her?"

"Oh, stop it momma. It's just a big ole coincidence. That's all."

Twila fidgeted with her keys, trying hard not to engage her grandmother and her talks about what it means to have people you know die around you. *Death comes in three... let's get the holy water out...* Twila was in no mood for all that.

"Yeah, if you say so but I know better. We need to take that child to church with us first thing Sunday morning and have pastor pray over her."

"Well, a good prayer is good for everybody, but she doesn't have nothing wrong with her momma. Are you thirsty? Do you want something to drink?"

"Yeah, some of your good lemonade will do me just fine."

Twila looked over at her mother and smirked, her mother gave her the same smile. The "I got it handled" smile that they sometimes had to give when grandma was on everyone's nerves. Maddie walked into the living room and stood by the door, her tail wagging wildly. "Who is at the door Maddie?" Twila soothed and walked over and stood next to her dog. "Uh, ma. Did you know daddy was on his way over here?"

"Yep, he wanted to stop by and see how you were feeling after the funeral."

"Okay." Twila picked Maddie up and opened the door for her father. "Hi Daddy."

"Hey Dumplin'. How are you feeling?" He asked while petting Maddie behind the ears before walking into the house.

"I'm ok. Just tired."

"Hey there Fred."

"Ms. Shirley, hey," her dad spoke and looked over at Twila's mother, giving her the side eye. "I didn't know you were here, or I would've brought you something."

"Oh, it's alright baby. Save your money for that little young wife you got—"

"So, Fred. What's up? How are you doing today? Would you like some lemonade?" Twila and her mother both flashed her father the "I got it handled" look.

"Yes, I'd love some," he replied and smiled back, thanking them both quietly. Maddie ran to the back door and began to bark, catching everybody off guard.

"You want to go outside girl? Come on."

Twila watched her mother interact with her dog, smiling at them both.

"I see your momma is getting used to having Maddie around, huh?"

"Yeah, she is. I think she likes her more than she says," Twila chuckled.

"Yeah, so, how's Josh handling everything?"

Twila thought of the secret meeting amongst the coach and all his victims after the funeral. No one but the team was invited. *Maybe I should tell daddy*, she thought quietly. "He's taking it ok," she said instead.

"That's good. I know it has to be hard losing not only one but two teammates in less than a year."

Twila pivoted in her seat. "Yeah, I guess so."

"How's the investigation going Fred? Anything new?" Sharon asked as she handed Fred his drink and sat down on the other side of the couch.

Twila's gut flipped as she waited for her father to respond.

Taking a drink of his lemonade, Twila's dad smiled. "This is good. You make the best lemonade in the world."

"*Get to it dad*," Twila mumbled internally.

"Thanks, I still got it," Sharon replied.

"Well, nothing has come up. Nothing unusual anyway. We have to rule it an accidental death," he said before taking another swig of his drink.

Twila went numb. *Accidental... The coach is going to get off.*

"Oh, my Lord," Twila's grandmother called out. "The poor boy. I pray that his family comes to terms with it all and be able to rest a little more comfortably now that there was no foul play or anything."

"Right, but it makes me wonder," Fred stopped and drank more of his drink before continuing. "I wonder how many other kids are using steroids. There was so much in his system when he died. I can only hope and pray that more high school kids aren't taking that stuff."

Twila looked up to find both her parents looking at her. "What?" she quipped.

"Have you heard anything about kids using steroids at school?" Her mother asked.

"Yeah," her father joined in. "Is there anything we need to know about?"

Twila stood up and stretched, walking out of the living room and to the back door to let her dog in. "Not that I know of," she said calmly, surprising herself.

"So, Josh hasn't said anything to you about using steroids?" Her mother crossed her arms and asked.

"Not only that stuff but any kind of drug," her grandmother cut in.

"No, nothing."

"Well, have you asked him?"

"Daddy, no. Why would I ask Josh something like that?"

"Just wondering Dumplin', that's all. Have you ever seen Josh act—"

"Daddy, I just came home from a friend's funeral. Can we skip the interrogation please?" Twila softened her tone and smiled at her father. "Just a long day, you know."

"Yeah, Dumplin', I get it."

Close call. "I'm going to head upstirs for a while and take a nap. I'm pretty tired. I will call you when I wake up dad."

"Alright baby girl."

"Grandma, I love you." Walking over to her grandmother, Twila kissed her on the cheek.

"Love you too baby," her grandmother said and smiled.

Twila hugged her father before walking up the stairs to her room, Maddie walking close behind her.

CHAPTER 21

Twila, Adriana, and Josh all stood at a standstill; not sure on how to proceed. "Josh, you are the one who's been hurt by the coach's actions. You have to tell my father."

"Twila, I already told you, I can't do that. I can and will be in a lot of trouble if I go to your father and tell him about the coach. The coach is doing everything for our own good. He knows how bad most of us need a scholarship so we doing what we gotta' do."

"Josh, what did y'all talk about at y'all secret meeting the other day after the funeral?"

Adriana asked while throwing Josh's football up in the air and catching it.

"Why?" Josh angrily huffed. "That's none of your business."

"A'ight, dang. I was just asking."

"How do you even know about that?" Josh looked over at Twila eyeing her intently.

Twila shook her head and looked out onto the sidewalk at Ariel riding her bike.

"Josh!"

Josh sighed and looked up towards the sky. "Ma'am?"

"Don't forget to take this trash out! It's been sitting in here all day!"

"Yes ma'am," Josh replied to his mother but remained seated on the porch.

"And don't forget that I will be checking to make sure that room is cleaned."

"Yes ma'am."

The pamphlets sprang into Twila's mind. "Josh?"

"Yeah," Josh answered.

If I ask him, then he would know that I've been in his room, searching around. Then it would be another reason for him not to trust me. "Nothing. Never mind."

"What?" Josh asked, looking over at her.

"Nothing," Twila chuckled uncomfortably.

Adriana looked at Twila and frowned. "Since when have you been scared to ask a question?"

"I'm not, I was just going to ask a dumb question but decided not to, that's all."

"Yeah right... okay."

Twila gave Adriana the side eye and looked back out onto the sidewalk. Although the sun shined brightly, Twila was seeing nothing but clouds and gloom within her surroundings. *What kind of person am I to just sit back and do nothing about the coach killing James?* She thought to herself. *What kind of girlfriend am I to let Josh stay around his coach knowing that he could potentially suffer the same fate as James?*

"Hey girls," Josh's mother cheerfully spoke as she came onto the porch.

"Hi, Ms. Trina," Twila and Adriana said in unison.

"Twila, don't forget, I have a book that I want to send to your mom so let me know when you're leaving."

"Okay."

Twila watched Trina as she watered her flower garden. *Maybe I can hint to Ms. Trina that something is going on with the football team. Maybe she can... What am I thinking? If Ms. Trina knows and she knew that I know all about it, she would never trust me again.*

"Adriana, how've you been dear?"

"Pretty good," Adriana smiled.

"Well, that's good baby. Glad to hear that you're doing well."

"Thanks."

"Be sure to tell your parents that I said hello."

"Yes ma'am, will do."

"Mommy!"

"Yes baby?"

"I want to go to the park!"

"You do! Well, I'm busy right now love. Maybe later."

"I can take her Ms. Trina," Twila said, eager to get off the porch and to clear her mind off all the drug stuff that crowded it. Josh looked at Twila and then at his mother. Adriana stood and gathered her belongings.

"Okay, thanks Twila."

"No problem."

"Josh, you coming?"

"Uh, nah, I got to go to practice."

"Practice? I didn't know you had practice today," Trina looked up.

"Yeah, me neither," Twila said, frowning.

Adriana chuckled and walked off the porch. "Another secret meeting," she said under her breath.

"Josh, can't you just skip practice today and come with us to the park?"

"Nope, gotta' go. I will hit you later."

"Ma, I will be back in a little while."

"Okay baby," Trina said as she continued to water her flowers.

Twila's heat sank as she watched Josh hug his sister and walk off.

"Faster Twila! Faster!" Ariel squealed as Twila pushed her on the swings.

"What do you think Josh is doing right now?" Adriana asked.

Twila sighed and pushed Ariel higher on the swings. "I don't know. I hope it's not what I think."

"Twila, girl, you know that's exactly what is going on. I talk to Dwayne earlier and he said that they didn't have practice today, so you know what it is."

"What? Adriana!"

"What?"

"Why didn't you say that before Josh left?"

"Uh, what would've been the point? Josh would've still left, and it would've caused a mess between you and him; not to mention a mess between him and his mom."

Twila continued to push Ariel on the swings. "You got a point... but still!"

"Girl, I ain't got time to deal with Josh and his attitude. That's yo' man. If he wants to do the med—"

"Shhh," Twila interrupted and pointed at Ariel.

"Ariel, do you want to go and play on the sliding board for a while? I think I see Amber over there."

"Amber? Where?"

"Over there. By the sliding board."

"Yeah," Ariel said and jumped off the swing, anxious to get to her classmate. "Amber!" She called out.

"Now, what were you saying?" Twila walked over to the closest bench and sat down, signaling for Adriana to join her.

"It's his life girl, let 'em live it how he wants. Let all them boys live how they want to live."

"Adriana, one of *those* boys died," Twila huffed. "Dead. I can see if it was something like... like dressing crazy or... playin' girls... something like that but we are talking about stuff that can kill. We have proof of that. James left behind a kid... two kids!"

"Hmmm, messin' with a bunch of girls can kill too, especially at our school," Adriana laughed. "I think you need to say out of it. Josh will be graduating soon anyway; problem solved."

"Yeah and I would love to see him participate in the graduation instead of being a part of the memorial during it." Twila looked over at Ariel and smiled. "She's so adorable and she needs her brother. It's bad enough their father isn't around. It would be messed up if she had to grow up without her father and her brother."

"Yeah. I feel you on that. Maybe you should try calling Josh; if his phone rings, then maybe his coach would stop, and you can talk some sense into him."

"I tried that. He doesn't answer when he's with his coach." *Yeah but you never walked in on him.* A bright lightbulb went off in Twila's head. "Uh, A, could you take Ariel home for me? I'm going to go—"

"No, don't do that. Don't go to the scene of the crime. Girl, what is wrong with you?"

"I have to. Maybe if the coach finds out that more people know, then he would stop."

"Okay, do what you feel is best but keep your phone with you. Call me if you need me."

"Thanks girl."

"Yep, go on and I will go ahead and take Ariel home."

Wasting no time, Twila stood up and went on her way, thinking of how she was going to confront the football coach.

He needs to be smacked, Twila whispered as she stood by the entrance to the gym and spied on the coach. She couldn't hear them; all she could do was see the look of desperation on his face and the look of worry on the boys'. Looking closer, she even spotted looks of hatred sprinkled in the crowd. Gasping, she leaned back as the coach looked around and then back at his team. Seeing Josh, a tinge of hurt spilled into her stomach. "Oh Josh," she mouthed. A change in position from the crowd grabbed Twila's attention causing her to focus her eyes a bit sharper. The boys lined up in a single file line as the coach continued to talk. The coach looked around the gym and towards the entrance and again, Twila leaned back just in time before she was caught. "He is so wrong for..." Twila's voice trailed off as she noticed a visitor entering from the back of the gym; the office area. A mop of white hair came into view. "Oh... my... gosh... Coach Snow!" She hissed. Twila began to feel hot and dizzy at the sight of Coach Snow pulling out a needle and injecting one of the boys.

CHAPTER 22

O kay, I've been telling you guys to study all month long," Ms. Engelman fussed. "Only a few actually took my advice and did it."

I'm not in the mood for this today, Twila sighed as she sat in her seat and hoped that time would be kind and move along faster than usual. Not only was Coach Davis and his fiasco with the drugs on her mind, but Coach Snow had a seat right next to his. They both caused her brain to be unnecessarily overcrowded; thoughts of schoolwork and Josh were already crammed in pretty tight before they got in. *I can't believe*

Coach Snow is involved in all this. That's crazy to me.

"Twila?"

At the sound her name, both coaches, Josh, and her schoolwork all puffed away as she looked towards the person who had called her.

"Yes?"

"Aren't you going to go to your next class? Or do you plan to stay in here with me? I can always use the company."

"Sorry," she muttered and began to assemble her belongings.

"You feeling alright today?"

Twila rushed to put her books in her book bag. "Yes ma'am, I'm good," she lied.

"Okay, well, looks like you're going to be late. I'll write you a pass."

"Thanks," Twila mumbled as Ms. Engelman walked towards her desk.

Wya, a text from Adriana popped onto her phone, looking at it, she hit the mute button and stood up, grabbed her pass and headed to her next class, silent as ever.

"Finally!" Twila quipped as she practically ran out of her English class. Yes, English was her favorite subject, but she just wasn't feeling school at the moment.

"Aye, what happened to you earlier? I texted you."

"Hey girl, Ms. Engelman held the class up earlier, so I had to rush to get to English class. Was sup?!" *As cheerful as I can be,* she thought as she walked towards the big double doors that seemed to shine the closer, she got to them. "I've been wanting to go home all day!"

"I feel you, me too. What are you doing later? I have to work but I thought maybe we can hang out for a little while after I get off. That's if you're not babysitting."

"Sure, I'm free tonight. I have some homework, but I will be finish by the time you get off. Just call—"

"Hey! Twila!"

Twila and Adriana both stopped and turned around.

"Girl, why is he calling your name all loud?"

"Because we are in the hallway, I guess."

"Hey," Josh said and hugged Twila. "Aye, I need to talk to you for a minute."

"Um, okay. Was sup?"

"Nah, not here; Come with me for a minute."

Twila looked at Adriana and then back at Josh. "Go with you where? Why can't we just talk right here or go to—"

"'Cause, I want to show you something. Come on."

Twila looked at Adriana again, wondering if she'd noticed the same thing that she had, Josh was acting really funny. *Is it the steroids?*

"You want me to go with you? My mom is picking me up today and she is slow, so I got some time."

"No, just Twila."

"Why?" Twila said in a confused tone.

"Yeah, what is wrong with—"

"A'ight, okay, just come on. Always arguing and fussing about something."

A doomed feeling burned within Twila's gut. Choosing to ignore it, she followed Josh down the long hallway that lead to the locker rooms.

"How did I know we were going here?" Adriana sarcastically quipped.

The group remained quiet as Josh pulled open the boys' locker room.

"Why there? Ain't the football team in there changing or something?"

"No, Adriana. Just come on," Josh angrily answered.

Adriana smacked her lips and nudged Josh. Josh continued to walk, ignoring Adriana.

Walking into the room, Twila kept her eyes straight ahead, knowing that the next person she saw would undoubtedly be the crooked coach. *Would it be Coach Davis alone or would he have his equally crooked side kick with him, Coach Snow?* And there he was, standing there looking like the devil himself. Walking closer, Twila looked Coach Davis in the eyes but didn't say a word. She stood still and waited for him to speak.

"Hi, can I speak with you for a sec?" Her moment; the moment she waited for since she found out that he was drugging his team to compensate for the head star, Kyle's death.

"Huh? About what?" She played dumb. She knew full well what he wanted to talk about.

"Um, no," Adriana said and put her arm around her friend.

"Adriana, mind your business," Josh said, breaking the weird silence that fogged up the room.

"Twila *is* my business!" Adriana shot back while looking at both Coach Davis and Josh, daring either of them to challenge her.

Coach Davis stared at Adriana for a few seconds before focusing his attention on Twila. "Twila, I know that you know about my team's sacrifice and I'm asking you to please keep it to yourself. I'm doing it for my boys' good. You can understand that, right?"

Twila wanted to smack him. Of course, she was taught to always respect her elders but as far as she was concerned, Coach Davis was the exception.

"Nope, I don't understand!" She blurted out. A weight as heavy as ten cement blocks lifted off her shoulders. "You are *killing* your *boys* not helping them!"

Coach Davis put his hand on his head and sighed. "Of course, you wouldn't understand. We just plan to give them a boost just until the end of the season and then we are stopping it for good. No harm done."

Twila looked at the coach as if he had tentacles coming out of his face. "No harm done, no harm. Do you remember James? You should; we just attended his funeral and you just killed him!"

"Now... wait!"

"No, you wait! What you're doing is wrong! You need to stop it!" Adriana put her hand on Twila's back and eyed the coach intently.

"Okay, here's the deal. I didn't want to go there, but it looks like I have to."

Twila frowned and waited for the coach to continue.

"If you don't drop everything and forget what you saw I will make your remaining years here at Harriet High miserable. Got that?!"

"Excuse me?" Twila said harshly and looked over at Josh. She was appalled to see that her boyfriend had his head down, not saying a word to defend her.

"You heard me. Don't make trouble for us and we won't make trouble for you. Simple."

"Did a teacher just threaten a student?" Adriana asked loudly. Twila couldn't believe her ears. *This man just threatened me.* With that, she looked at Adriana and the two of them walked away.

CHAPTER 23

Why do they even bother? I mean, what is this, really?" Adriana frowned at the blob of mashed potatoes lined unevenly in the long rectangular pain in the school lunch line. "Hey? Was sup? Why are you so quiet today?"

"Just stuff on my mind," Twila responded before grabbing her tray and walking out of the line to a seat.

"What kind of... oh, him," Adriana pointed. Twila followed Adriana's motion and frowned. "Yup, him." Adriana shook her head and flopped down on the seat.

"Twila, you need to let him go. Too much on your mind is a bad thing."

Twila sat down across from Adriana and pushed her tray to the side, replacing the space with her English composition book. Thinking about the pamphlets she'd seen in Josh's room rattled her; not able to remove it completely from her mind. Glancing over at him, she frowned as he laughed and threw a football around with his teammates. *Oh, so he's all good with his friends but not with me. Okay, I feel 'em. Time for me to get my mind off him.*

Rolling her eyes, she looked back at Adriana. "So, girl, Whatchu doing tonight?"

"Nothing, was sup?"

"Let's go chill at the mall."

"It's way too crowded in here for a Tuesday." Maneuvering through the crowd, Twila smacked her lips as a girl bumped into her.

"Excuse you!"

"Excuse you! You bumped into her!" Adriana griped.

"Adriana, stop. Don't start no mess."

"I'm not startin' nothing. She started it by running her mouth!"

Twila pulled Adriana by the arm. "Come on girl." Twila looked behind her, glad that the girls had went on their way. "Come on, let's sit over here for a minute. Maybe they will clear out of here soon. It's not usually busy this time of the week." Twila sat down on the seat and crossed her legs as she watched the crowds of people walk by, laughing and talking amongst each other.

"I don't know where all these people are coming from."

Twila laughed. "Adriana, you need to calm down. It's a mall so it shouldn't be completely empty."

"Yeah, but it shouldn't be this crowded either."

"I guess," Twila muttered and continued looking around the mall. Her mind reverted back to Josh and the way he'd acted in the gym with his coach. *I can't believe he is acting like such a sellout.*

"So, what is going on with the boy you are *still* calling your boyfriend?"

Twila sighed and shook her head. "Girl, I don't know. I'm tired of dealing with him and his mess. I can't believe how he's been acting lately."

"I can! Twila, I told you before that you need to dump him and find someone else. There are plenty of boys at school that you can talk to. Most of them are lame, but they are available. Why don't you start talking to one of them?"

"Why would I do that if they are all lames?"

"True."

The girls remained quiet for a few seconds as they both watched a lady and her young daughter argue over which store to go into. The mother gave in and hastily walked into the toy store; the child happily ran inside. Twila chuckled, "Reminds me of Ariel."

"Yeah, she does act like the little brat. Come on, let's go in there. It beats sitting out here on the bench doing nothing."

"If you call her a brat one more time, I'ma—"

"Shut up and come on."

Twila followed Adriana into the toy store. Playfully pushing Adriana, she smiled at the array of colors; toys for all different ages lined the shelves.

"You remember this?"

Twila laughed at the black ball Adriana held in her hands.

"Yeah, the eight ball. I remember that."

Adriana giggled and placed it back on the shelf.

Walking around in the store didn't help with Twila's thoughts. Her mind was still deeply on Josh and the fact that he didn't protect her.

Maybe I should dump him. Who needs a boyfriend like that?

"Get your mind off him girl, he is not worth the thought."

"I know A, but I can't help it. My mind is on all the stuff that happened with him," Twila replied while picking up a stuffed animal, rubbing it, and placing it back on the shelf.

"I don't know-"

"Hey, excuse me?"

Twila and Adriana looked over at the security guard staring down at them. "Um, yes?" Twila spoke softly.

"I need to speak with the both of you for a moment. Step over here please."

"For what?!" Adriana spat

"I will answer all of your questions once we are over in my office. Either we can go to my office or we can talk here."

Twila thought of her father's words when it came to the law; always obey and call me as soon as you get with them. "We will go to your office and then I need to call my father," Twila responded and looked over at Adriana, pleading with her to keep her mouth shut.

"Okay, it's this way."

Twila looked around the store, *something doesn't seem quite right. Why is this security guard leading us to his office? For what and what did we do?* The cashiers were still ringing customers up, not bothering to pay any attention to anything else. Everything seemed to be in order in the store except for the fact that Twila and Adriana were the only two being led away for nothing at all. Finally reaching a small room with a tiny light and two chairs, Twila sat down and pulled out her phone.

"Whoa! Hold on a minute!"

"I need to call my—"

"I know, I know, and you will have the chance but first I want to have a conversation on why you two are in here."

Twila sat back in her seat as Adriana stood up.

"We need to get out of here! We didn't do anything!" Adriana huffed.

"Oh really?"

"That's right," Adriana replied. "So, we need to go!"

"Well I got you two on video camera putting something in your pockets."

"What?!" Twila blurted out. "What do you mean? We didn't put anything in our pockets. What are you talking about?"

The guard sat in his seat, unbothered by Twila's reaction. Adriana sat down next to Twila and put her head down.

"I need to call my dad, please."

"No need. I have someone here who is willing to pay for the items that you put into your pocket."

"I did not put anything in my pocket and neither did my friend!" Twila yelled.

"Relax."

Twila watched in horror as the security guard picked up the radio and called something into it. "I cannot believe this is happening," she mumbled. The room grew uncomfortably silent before someone knocked on the door.

"Come on in!"

Twila gasped and Adriana shook her head in disbelief as Coach Davis walked into the room. "What is he doing here?!" Adriana huffed. In an instant, everything snapped into place in Twila's mind.

"He's here to threaten us in some way," Twila said and stood up.

"No, no, nothing like that. Have a seat."

"Thanks, Mark. I owe you one."

"Are you serious?!" Adriana said to the security guard. "You got us up in here for him?" she pointed hastily at the coach.

Mark shook the coach's hand and walked out of the room, not saying a word as he left.

"I just wanted to make sure we were clear about our conversation."

"Really? So, you go through all this trouble just to make sure we won't tell on you! I don't have time for this!"

"Sit down, Adriana! You know, you really don't have anything to do with this. So I'ma just speak with Twila and then the two of you can go."

"This is crazy," Twila was meaning to say to herself but it came out loudly.

"You're right; it is crazy, and it can all go away if you just promise me that you will keep your mouth shut."

Twila looked at Coach Davis and chuckled. "If you don't let me go; let us go, I will get my father in here and you will go down pretty fast."

"Right!" Adriana followed Twila's lead.

Twila stood up, grabbed Adriana's arm and walked out of the office. Rolling her eyes at Mark, Twila and Adriana walked as fast as they could out of the toy store.

"Can you believe that?! I mean, is he really in that deep that he has to follow us to the mall and have somebody trap us in an office so he can come and threaten us some more. What is wrong with that man?" The people walking around, and the stores lined up in the mall were now just a big blur to Twila. Anxious to get home, she and Adriana both said nothing as they walked out of the mall and into Adriana's dad's car.

CHAPTER 24

"Twila, come on back dear." Twila walked past a couple of students who were waiting to be suspended due to a fight in the cafeteria earlier before reaching Ms. Hanks' office. "Come on in and have a seat," the principal smiled. "Tell me, what can I help you with sweetie?"

The threat from the coach flooded her mind but her mouth wasn't working. The exact moment she needed it to work, it wouldn't move.

"Twila?"

"Uh, I just wanted to ask a question."

"Okay. Sure. Can I get you some water?"

"No... no, I'm okay." *Just ask it Twila*! Her inner voice yelled. "Um," she started. "What happens if a teacher is mean to a student?" *Really? Did you really just ask that? He wasn't just mean, he threatened you!* Her voice continued. *Talk!* "Not just mean," she continued.

Ms. Hanks sat up in her seat, giving Twila her undivided attention.

"Not just mean but threatens. What happens if a teacher threatens a student?" *There, it's out.*

"Threaten? Twila, did a teacher threaten you?"

"Oh no! No, I was just wondering and asking for a friend."

Ms. Hanks lifted her eyebrows and put her hand on her desk. "I do not take threats lightly. Is it someone here at our school?"

Twila looked towards the ceiling before she answered. "Yes," she said.

Ms. Hanks stood up, walked towards the door and called out. "Ms. Rivington, could you please come in here for a moment?"

"Be right there!"

Why is she calling in Ms. Rivington?

"We will get to the bottom of this. Who was the teacher?"

"Teachers," Twila quickly answered.

"Oh really?"

"Yes ma'am. Well, it was only one of them who threatened me... I mean my friend."

"Twila, you can talk to me. I'm here to help you," Ms. Hanks said and sat down next to Twila. "It's time to admit that you are talking about yourself."

Feeling a bit more comfortable, Twila was ready to talk, to speak her peace and let it all out. "Coach Davis—"

"Yes ma'am," Ms. Rivington walked in.

"Ms. Rivington, I need you to get me the paperwork to file a complaint. We have a teacher who threatened a student and I would like this handled as soon as possible."

"Okay, be right back."

Ms. Hanks' eyes followed her assistant until she was at her desk, searching through her file cabinet.

"Coach Davis?"

"Huh?"

"Before Ms. Rivington walked in, you mentioned Coach Davis."

The feelings of boldness had suddenly turned to mush. Twila began to feel hot and dizzy, just as she felt when she noticed that not only was Coach Davis involved in illegal activity, but her own gym teacher, Coach Snow, was right in the middle of it too. "Um..." she managed to mutter.

"Twila, go ahead and tell me what's going on. It has to be pretty serous for you to come in here in the first place."

Twila sighed, not sure if she should open this huge can of worms. *The entire school could go down if the police are called...if my daddy is called.*

"Twila?"

"Coach Davis... he's been giving the team meds." Twila closed her eyes and continued. "Steroids." It felt like she'd waited hours for her principal to respond although it was only minutes.

"Okay."

"Okay?"

"Yeah, it's all good. You know Twila, we are a family here at Harriet High and we would do nothing at all to hurt each other. I promise you..." Stopping halfway through, Ms. Hanks walked over to the door and closed it. "I can promise you that the meds that Coach Davis is giving is perfectly ok. Just a small boost to help the guys stay on track. Nothing to worry about."

Twila was absolutely dumbfounded. There were no words to express exactly how she was feeling.

"Now you said he threatened you. How? What did he say?"

Twila looked at her principal and stood up. "It was nothing; just a misunderstanding," she said before getting up, looking back at Ms. Hanks and walking out without saying another word.

"Twila, if you want to continue to get good grades in this class, I'm going to need you to do more! Move those legs!"

"Dang! It's just gym class," Twila said to herself as she stopped, stretched, and began to jog again. *I ain't killing myself because she thinks everybody should be like her.* Stopping mid-way, she stretched her arms and her legs again and stood still, allowing the other girls in her class to go ahead of her.

"Hey Twila," one of her classmates spoke while jogging past her.

"Hey girl," Twila replied. Looking out in the field behind her school, Twila took notice of the houses and the trees that lined them. A nature person by heart, her father always described her as being so, and she'd come to know that as being true. It was something about the simple beings of nature that seemed to captivate her. Especially when she didn't want to be somewhere like gym class. *I don't even know why we have to do this. Why is this even a grade?* Twila continued to look out at her surroundings while she walked slowly on the track. Zoning in on a milk truck pulling in behind the cafeteria kept her mind off the walk; anything to keep her mind off the task at hand. Watching two men hop out of the truck, laughing and talking, she frowned when she saw Coach Davis walk out of the cafeteria. *I just don't like him. Having him here only makes this school so much worse than what it is.* She smacked her lips as Coach Davis laughed aloud at something one of the men had said. *Such a jerk.* Passing a few other kids who decided to take her lead and catch a quick break while Coach Snow was yelling at some of the boys from the football team. Twila chuckled but kept it moving, deciding that it is in her best interest to do so. *I don't feel like hearing her mouth again today.* Walking along the track, she noticed more kids just standing around. Looking behind her, she was now the only one walking. They better come on before she goes ape—

"Twila! Come on in! It's time to hit the showers."

Twila looked around again, noticing that she was now the only one on the field, except for a couple of girls standing a few feet away from her.

"Twila! Let's go girl!"

Twila rolled her eyes and began jogging towards Coach Snow.

"You are slow today girl!"

"Yeah," Twila muttered and walked into the locker room. When did everybody get in here? She mumbled as all of her classmates were in the locker room. Some were talking amongst each other, some were in the shower, and others were already dressed and waiting on the bell to ring.

"Hey Twila! You going to the school's picnic this year?"

"No, I don't think so."

"Why not? I think they are having another dance off during it, you should enter. Is Adriana going?"

Twila looked up at the girl who was talking to her but for some reason, she didn't know who the girl was. Not wanting to be rude and tell her that she didn't know her, she just smiled. "Maybe, I will have to ask her."

"Okay, dat's was sup," the girl said and trotted off towards the other side of the locker room.

Who was that? Twila whispered. I've never seen her around here before.

"Hey girl, you still sitting here? What is taking you so long to get dressed so we can get out of here. My dad will be here in a minute."

"Adriana? What are you doing in here? You don't have gym this—"

"I'm here to get your slow butt. Now come on so we can go and wait for my dad...Outside. You know I don't like it in here."

Twila laughed, stood up and stretched.

"Adriana, was sup girl."

"Hey Anna."

Twila frowned at the exchange between Adriana and the girl who asked her about the school's picnic and Adriana a few minutes prior. *Anna,* she whispered. *Who's Anna?*

"I was asking Twila were you going to the picnic this year. You know they are supposed to have another dance off again this year. You and Twila should enter; they are having teams."

"Okay, maybe we will."

"Okay, see you later."

Adriana smiled and Twila was confused. "A, who was that? I have no idea on who she is."

"You know Anna."

"No, I don't remember being a student—"

"From elementary school. You know the one with the braces."

Twila laughed. "Adriana, there were a lot of kids with braces."

"Yeah but the one who got them first."

Twila remembered her face but just couldn't place her being a student at Harriet. *Maybe I just overlooked her. But then how does she know me and how does Adriana know her?*

"You know, the one they called tracks."

"Uh, um, okay," Twila agreed, just to end the conversation.

"Come on, let's go outside and wait for my dad."

"Okay," Twila replied and walked closely beside Adriana.

A large group of boys walked past causing Twila to feel uncomfortable. She couldn't place why she felt that way but something about them made her feel extremely uneasy. Reaching the hallway, the lights were dimly lit for a school day and all the doors to the classrooms were closed.

"Are you babysitting tonight?"

Twila continued to look around her school; her very unfamiliar school. "Yes, I have to sit with Ariel while Ms. Trina takes her finals."

"Oh, I was thinking we can go to the mall or something."

"Maybe I can go after Ms. Trina gets back home or if Josh comes home early or something."

"Well, I doubt if Josh gets done early. I heard they were having practice late tonight. His mom will most likely be home by the time they finish."

"How would you know—"

"Twila! Come here! You got to see this!"

Twila looked towards the sound of the voice only to find the same girl, whom she didn't know, staring at her from down the hall. *Who is this girl! I feel like I know her but just not from school.* "What is it?" Twila yelled back with a voice full of uncertainty.

"You have to come down here!"

"Adriana..." Twila's voice trailed off. *Where in the world did she go*? Adriana!" She called out. Looking around in the hallway, she noticed that not only was the dim lights off, but some of the lockers were ajar. *What is going on in here today and where is Adriana? Maybe she went outside.*

"Twila! You coming?! Tracks wants to show us something and it is crazy!"

"Tracks? Really? Adriana when did you get down there?! I thought you—"

"Just come on or you'll miss it! You got to see this!" Adriana laughed and then disappeared behind the door to one of the biology labs.

Twila reluctantly walked down the hall to meet Adriana. *Something is not right. Something just doesn't feel right.* Ignoring her thoughts and her feelings, she moved along anyway.

"Hurry up, Twila!" Adriana called out again.

"Man, I got to see this!" A boy ran past Twila, almost knocking her down.

"What is so good about what's going on in the lab?"

"Twila, was sup girl. You still talk to Josh?"

"Hi, yep," she answered quickly to one of the boys she recognized from her English class.

"Dat's was sup. I was going to ask you to chill wit' me this weekend but since you still with Josh..."

"Aye! Wait up!" He yelled at a couple of boys that were walking ahead of him.

Chill with him? Twila frowned in confusion as the boy disappeared out of her sight. *Why is he talking to me? He doesn't say anything to me in class or even when he sees me in the halls any other time so why now?*

Sighing, she continued her walk to the lab to see what Adriana wanted.

"Twila! Come on girl!" Adriana poked her head out of the classroom.

"I'm coming! What is going on in there that you want me to see so badly?"

Adriana ran out of the room and pulled Twila's arm. "Come on!"

Twila allowed Adriana to lead her in the room. Frowning, she looked over at Adriana. "This is what you called me in here to see. A bunch of boxes stacked everywhere."

"It's what's inside that counts. Go look!"

"Yeah, go and look inside!" The other kids followed.

Twila walked over to one of the boxes and peeked inside. She gasped at the sight of large blue balloons and what looked like thousands of syringes packed in between each one of the balloons. "What is—"

"Hold her down!"

Twila turned to run but was quickly grabbed by Coach Davis and Ms. Hanks.

"Hold her down, Coach!" Ms. Hanks yelled."

"This one is too strong!" Coach Davis replied, taking Twila's arm and twisting it.

"Ow!" Twila yelled. "Get off of me!"

"Sorry, Twila but you couldn't keep your mouth shut. Just had to go to Ms. Hanks and make her all nervous so now you get what you're going to get!"

"Adriana! Call my dad!" Twila caught a glimpse of Adriana and was dumbfounded with the laughter that was plastered on her face and coming out of her mouth. "What?!" She stammered before she was taken down by Coach Davis.

"I got this!" Josh yelled from the doorway.

"Josh! Please help me! Josh!"

"I got you Twila; just hold on."

"Let her go!"

To Twila's surprise, both Coach Davis and Ms. Hanks let her go without saying another word, giving Josh full control of the situation.

"Josh! Thank God!" Twila yelled as Josh pushed Coach Davis and Ms. Hanks off her. "Thank God you are here!"

"Come on, let's go."

A rush of relief gripped Twila as she and Josh reached the door and ran out.

"You good?"

Twila hugged Josh. "Yeah, I'm good. I'm-"

"There you are!"

Twila turned away from Josh to see her stepmother walking quickly towards her. "Candice, what are you doing...? What is that?" Twila cringed at the long needle in Candice's hand.

"Hold her Josh!"

"I got her; just go ahead with it!" Josh yelled.

"What are y'all doing?!"

"Twila this is for your own good," Candice spoke in an unusual calming voice. "You need to know how well the steroids are working for the football team. If you know just how much they need it, then maybe you would stop telling people about it."

Josh held Twila down as Candice pulled the cover off the needle.

"Noooo!" Twila screamed and jolted awake just before Candice had the chance to stick her with the needle. Picking and prodding on her body, she was happy and relieved that she was free of holes; free of steroids and the whole thing was just a dream. "That was crazy," she whispered while flipping the light on beside her on the nightstand. Everything was in its usual space and Maddie was sound asleep on her side in her cage. Twila reflected on her dream and even though she was awake, it still scared her. Sitting up in bed, she slipped her feet off the bed and lightly stretched before getting completely up and standing. Taking another peek at Maddie, she walked out of her room and into the hallway. Looking in her mother's bedroom, she saw that her mom was asleep, with the T.V on. The nightly news stared at her as she slept. *You always forget to turn the T.V off.* Walking down the stairs, she stopped in at the door to double check that it was locked. Thanks to the nightmare she'd just had, she wanted to check everything to be sure that she and her mom were safe. Assured that the door was locked, she walked over to the couch, turned the lamp on, and flopped down. Thinking of everything from Josh, Ms. Hanks, and the dream, there was no way she was going back to sleep. Flipping the T.V on, she plopped her feet up on the couch and skimmed through the channels, looking for nothing in particular, she ran across an old sitcom. Pulling her grandmother's old blanket off the recliner, she wrapped herself in it and finally began to feel comfortable. Chuckling, she watched a commercial for a cartoon fill the T.V. Watching for a few seconds, she flipped through the stations and stopped when she saw a familiar picture on the screen. An old yearbook picture of James stared back at her. Turning the volume up a little, she watched as a group of people discussed his life and drug use in schools.

You know, we need to take a look at schools and the use of drugs. A young man died and there seems to be nothing productive being done about it.

Twila immediately tuned out and put the T.V on mute. *I need to do something; I know what's going on and I should speak up.* Looking at the clock, she thought of her father, but by it being two in the morning, she was sure that he was sleeping. Or if he wasn't and was called into work on a case, he would be too busy to speak with her. Looking at the T.V., more pictures of James and his family flashed on the screen. Turning the T.V. completely off, she folded her grandmother's blanket, put the remote on the coffee table and decided to go back to bed. Going into her mother's room, she flipped her T.V off as well and headed to her bedroom. Glancing at Maddie, she smiled, noticing that Maddie was sleeping so well, that she was off her pillow and on the floor. *Humph, at least one of us is sleeping.* Pulling both her pillows over on her side of the bed, she grabbed her phone off the nightstand. "Ugh, why didn't I charge it before I went to bed?" Pulling her charger from the other side of the nightstand, she plugged her phone in, cut the light off, and tried hard not to think of the dream she'd had or the pictures she'd just seen on the news." James' story has now made national headlines," she sighed. *All the power lies in me. Everyone wants to know exactly what happened to him and I have some answers that would make everybody gasp.* Turning on her side, she closed her eyes. *I guess I should go back to doing what I was taught to do when I can't sleep, count sheep. One...Two...Three...*

So, are you going to the dance Friday night?" Twila pushed her hair back behind her ear and looked into the mirror. "I guess so. I haven't asked Josh yet."

"I don't think getting Josh's answer is a problem. What you're wearing is a different story," Adriana said while going through Twila's closet.

"Something simple. I'm not really feeling this...what did they call it?" Twila stood up and stretched. "*Ball* anyways. I probably won't even go. I'm definitely not feeling the school." Twila thought back to the day she had in the office with

Ms. Hanks. Deciding not to tell a soul, she kept the secret buried within her mind.

"Girl, you gotta' go. I need you there so I will have someone to talk to."

Twila chuckled. "Isn't that what your date is there to do?"

"Please, he ain't nobody. I'm just going with him because he seems so sad and I wanted to cheer him up. So, I need you there so I can keep my mind occupied."

"You are a crazy girl," Twila chuckled.

"Speaking facts. I don't like Jeremey like that, so I won't be paying him any attention."

The buzzing of the phone caught Twila's attention. Turning around she grabbed it and flopped down on her beanbag. "Hey, was sup?"

"Hey, Whatchu up to?"

"Chillin'."

"Listen, Twila. I'm sorry how things went down in the gym the other day. Coach is just a little worried about stuff; a lot of stuff on his mind."

"Yeah, okay. So, what are you doing tonight?"

"That's it? You not going to fuss me out or anything." *Nope, it's no need. Nobody is listening to Twila anyway. Why keep talking about it?* "Nope, none of that. You tryin' to go to the dance on Friday?"

"Yeah, that's cool. I'm trippin'."

Twila adjusted herself on her beanbag. "Why?" she chuckled.

"'Cause, you like all calm and stuff. I was thinking you was going to be all mad after what happened the other day."

"Why Josh? Nobody cares about what I'm saying so it's no need to keep talking about."

"I'm taking this."

Twila looked up at Adriana. "Girl put that back! That's my favorite romper."

"Well, it's going home with me for a while," Adriana chuckled.

"Oh, I didn't know you had company. I'll hit you later."

"Okay, talk to you later," Twila said and hung up on her end.

"You finally treating that boy like he needs to be treated. I'm glad you are finally acting like you got some sense!"

"Shut up and put my romper back where it belongs!" Twila spat.

"I will, just not today," Adriana giggled.

"Twila," her mother said while opening the bedroom door.

"Yes ma?"

"The principal just called and..."

"Oh, how are you doing Adriana?"

"Hi Ms. Sharon. I'm ok."

"That's good. I need to speak with Twila for a minute about something."

"Okay, it's getting late anyway so I will call my dad to pick me up."

"It's ok. Twila and I will take you home. Go on downstairs and get you some cookies. I baked some earlier," Sharon gave a warm smile.

"Thanks," Adriana replied while gathering her belongings. She snatched Twila's romper off the bed and licked her tongue out before walking out the door.

"She crazy," Twila laughed. "Was sup ma?"

"Well, your principal just called me and asked me to come in and speak with her in the morning. What's that all about?"

Twila stood up and walked over to her closet, thinking of the chat she and Ms. Hanks had about her coach and his football team.

"She called this time of night?"

"Yeah, strange huh? That's why I wanted to ask you about it. And I didn't want Adriana listening just in case it has something to do with her and her mess."

"Ma. Really? Why would Ms. Hanks call you and ask you to go to the school if it was something about Adriana? Wouldn't they call her mother or her father?"

"Because when Adriana had her problem, the guidance counselor called me and had some concerns about you."

"The guidance coun ...Ms. Gyles?"

"Hmm mmm, she said that she noticed some changes in you and that you and your "best friend" wasn't getting along. She was worried about you. I knew she had to be talking about Adriana and then we find out that she's an alcoholic."

"*Was* an alcoholic; she's not anymore."

"Right, well, *was*."

"Why didn't you tell me about that? Tell me that she called you?"

"Well, I don't have to tell you when a teacher or someone calls from school because once they call me, it is no longer on you but on me. So, that's one reason but I was going to talk to you and your father that night we found out about the mess with the accident. I figured your guidance counselor worries was old news after that."

"Huh?" Twila muttered.

"Now, why would your principal want to see me?"

This is the moment, *Twila... tell someone who actually has your back.* "I don't know," she shrugged her shoulders. "Maybe something about a project or something. I don't know."

"This late?"

"I have no idea ma," Twila chuckled, hoping to lighten the mood.

"Well, okay. I guess I will find out tomorrow. Maybe I should call your—"

"No!" Twila slumped as she noticed the surprised look on her mother's face. "I-I mean, no need to call daddy. You know how he can be."

Sharon stared at her daughter for a few seconds. "Yeah...ok... but I don't like that outburst. Looks like I need to keep your father on standby, just in case. Grab a sweater or something. It's chilly out." Twila waited for her mother to walk out of her room before she let the air that she'd been holding tight in her lungs out in a hearty exhale. *Why is Ms. Hanks calling my mom? I know she's not going to talk about all the illegal stuff she's allowing to go down so why does she need to see my mom?* Twila's mind was full of questions.

"Twila! Come one, it's getting late!"

Grabbing her jacket, she turned her lamp off and headed down the stairs.

"Took you long enough."

"Shut up, A. Did you tell your dad that we were bringing you home?"

"Yeah, I texted him and told him."

"Make sure Maddie's cage is locked. If I come back and find out she got out and bit my shoe again, I am going to get you and her."

Twila and Adriana laughed aloud while Twila secured her dog's cage.

"I will be back in a few girl," Twila cooed at her puppy.

Following Sharon outside, Twila and Adriana both zipped their jackets. "It is nippy out here," Sharon said while walking down the steps.

"Yeah it is. I got to close my—"

"What in the world is that?!" Sharon abruptly interrupted Adriana. Looking out in the yard, the ladies spotted a medium sized brown envelope.

"Looks like an envelope," Sharon said.

Adriana ran over to it and picked it up.

"Put that down Adriana! It could be dangerous!" Sharon yelled.

Adriana threw the envelope back onto the grass. Twila stood still, not sure on what to say or what to do.

"Twila, call your father. I will get him to check it out."

Daddy, why do we always have to call daddy? There are other officers that can help us sometimes. "Okay ma," she said instead, knowing better not to say her thoughts out loud.

"Ms. Sharon, It's a note on the back."

"A note?" Sharon said and walked over to Adriana. "What does it say?"

We know what is best. Stay out if it, Sharon read aloud. "What is this?" She said in a hoarse whisper as she looked over at Twila. Twila shrugged her shoulders.

"Maybe somebody dropped it," she answered. *Or maybe it's Coach Davis or his side kick, Coach Snow being all big and bold with it now.* Pulling her phone out of her pocket, she tapped her father's number.

"Why would somebody leave this in your yard?"

"I don't know Fred, that's why we called you...the big detective."

Fredrick looked at Sharon and then at Twila. "We know what's best... this has to mean some type of threat."

"Dad."

Fredrick looked up at Twila. "What? That's what this looks like. Do you have anything going on that—"

"No daddy. I am not beefin' with nobody. I don't have any problems anywhere."

"Humph. I see. Well, maybe somebody dropped it. I will hang on to it for a while; take it down to the station."

"Good idea and while you're playing police, I need you to meet me at the principal's office tomorrow."

"Playing police, ugh, I am the police," Fredrick chuckled.

"Yep, that you are." Sharon said and smiled sarcastically.

"What's going on at the principal's office?" Fredrick asked and glanced over at Twila. Twila shifted her wright and crossed her legs Indian style on the couch.

"I don't know. She called and asked me to meet her in her office in the morning. That's all I know."

"Alright, what time?"

"First thing. Come to think of it, she didn't say a time. Just asked me to meet her at her office."

Fredrick walked over to Twila, stopping to speak to Maddie on the way and sat down. "Dumplin', are you sure everything is ok at school?"

"Yep, all is well."

"What about personally?" Her mother chimed in.

"Ma, I promise. Everything is fine. Will you both please stop?" Twila sighed and leaned her head against the chair.

"Okay, but if I find out otherwise, you and I are going to have it out," Sharon said as she walked out of the living room.

"Okay Dumplin' I'm going to head out. Kissing his daughter on the cheek," Fredrick stood up and walked towards the living room door. "You call me if you need me."

"Yes daddy. I will."

"Okay, bye honey; bye Maddie."

Twila laughed as her dog looked up at the sound of her name and then put her head back down, inhaling deeply as she did.

CHAPTER 26

First, I want to thank you both so much for coming! Please, have a seat."

Twila and Ms. Hanks' eyes met before Twila sat down next to her father.

"Ms. Anderson, I love your earrings."

"Thanks. Now, what is this all about? You said you wanted to see me."

"Yes, right. I wanted to tell you personally that Twila will be our queen this year at our Spring ball! I wanted to tell you and Twila in person."

Twila looked up at her principal as if she had lost her mind. Looking at her mother, she shrugged her shoulders and then focused her attention back on Ms. Hanks. "Um..."

"Don't you have to be nominated for that kind of thing?" Her mother asked. Twila looked over at her father, noticing that he was at a complete lost.

"Yes, we do, and our school voted for Twila! Congratulations Twila!"

Twila sat back in her seat and gazed at her principal. *Really? This is all about your secret and you think making me queen at some dance will make it all go away.* "I don't want to," Twila blurted out. "Ma...dad...can we go? I have to babysit tonight."

"What's wrong, Dumplin'?"

Twila stood up and walked towards the door. "Thank you, Ms. Hanks, but no thanks," she said while opening the door.

"Twila! Get back here. What is the matter with you? Your principal called us in here to tell us in person that you were elected queen of the dance. Don't you think she deserves a little more respect?"

"Ma, it is a teacher's workday, so I need to get home and get ready to go and babysit."

"Twila, sit down."

Twila looked at her father and sighed, knowing that when he called her by her government name, he meant business.

"Thank you for coming in. I know it was short notice, but we like to inform our queens and kings in person once we find out who won the vote," Ms. Hanks said as she looked at Twila.

"Well, thank you for calling us," Sharon replied with a smile.

Twila watched both of her parents as they stood and shook Ms. Hanks' hand.

"Twila, I'll see you on Monday."

Twila looked at her principal and waved as she stood, happy that her parents were finally ready to go.

CHAPTER 27

U gh," Twila huffed while trying to put her right eyelash on. "I hate doing this! I don't know why I'm going to this stupid dance anyway."

"Oh, girl chill out. It's just an eyelash. Take it off and just don't wear any. Nothing wrong with wearing your natural ones."

Twila ignored Adriana as she continued to struggle with the daunting task. Growing more frustrated by the minute, Twila threw the eyelash down on the counter and surveyed herself in the bathroom mirror; admiring the blue ball gown she reluctantly picked out with her mother a few hours after Ms. Hanks informed them that she was Harriet's High queen of this year's ball. It fit as snug as a glove on her top half and flared out towards her bottom half, creating the perfect snow-white gown.

"Add more glue to it."

"Humph, if I add more glue, I will end up with blobs all over my lashes; looking like a clown instead of the queen."

"Yeah, I still can't get over how you're the queen this year. You never told me you entered," Adriana said while combing her edges down with the edge brush.

"I didn't enter. That's why I know it's more to this queen mess. I didn't enter and I don't remember voting for queen or kin... who is king this year?" Twila looked over at Adriana and frowned.

"Todd."

"Todd? Who's Todd?"

"You know Todd," Adriana replied as she added the finishing swirls to her edges. "Danica's cousin."

"Who would choose Todd?! All this is some crazy mess. First, I find out some stuff about the football team and now I'm... little ole me... is the queen of the spring ball. I've never been to the ball let alone being the queen of it this year! Then some lame dude is the king. None of this makes sense."

"Live It up girl! Enjoy yourself; it's only one night."

Twila huffed and picked up the halfway mangled eyelash and began to make attempts to put it on again. "Whatever, I'm just ready to get this over with."

"Hey girls! Ya'll both looks so pretty! Come on and let me take my pictures."

"Ma, can we wait to do the pictures until after I get my lashes on? I'm having trouble getting them on."

"Here, let me help you. Your father will be here soon, and you know he wants pictures."

Twila gave her mother the eyelash and adjusted her head, allowing her mother to help her.

"I don't know why you didn't call me in the first place. I would've popped this thing on a long time ago."

"Right," Twila sarcastically grunted.

"Got it! Now go on downstairs and let's wait for your father. The limo should be here soon too."

"Ugh! I feel like I have fans on my eyes! I hate these things!"

"I told you to not wear any," Adriana laughed. "There's nothing wrong with your natural eyelashes."

"Well, it's too late now. They are already on and I'm ready to go and get this mess over and done." Grabbing her blue heels, she walked behind Adriana and her mother, careful not to allow the weight of the dress to drag her and to make her fall. Halfway down the stairs, she looked at her shoes and frowned. Too much blue, she muttered and turned back towards her bedroom. Putting her shoes in its rightful box in her closet, she grabbed the box next to it and pulled a pair of opened toed sandal heels with crystal beading out and smiled. These are way too high, but I think they will look better with this dress. I just hope I don't fall again with these things on, she mumbled as thoughts of her slipping and falling, with the same exact shoes on her feet, at the eighth-grade graduation entered into her mind.

"Twila! Your dad is here, and Adriana's parents are here to take some pictures! Come on!"

Why is she always yelling? "I'm coming ma!" Making her way out of her room and slowly down the stairs, she smiled at the crowd of people waiting on her, they all had smiles on their faces like she was Beyoncé and they were getting ready to witness another masterful performance as only Beyoncé can bring.

"You look beautiful dumplin'."

"Thank you, daddy." Twila's eyes widened when she saw her mother's arched nemesis, Candice standing next to her father like she didn't have a care in the world. *I can't believe her, and ma are standing in the same space! In my house! In my mother's house!* Twila looked over at her mother as she made her way to the last step. *Okay, that's normal,* she chuckled internally as she noticed the shady look on her mother's face.

"Okay! Let's get these pictures done before the limo gets here. Twila! You still don't have your shoes on?! Girl what is going on with you?! You still don't have on your tiara! You're going to be-"

"Sharon, calm down. It's ok. Why don't we let Adriana's parents get some pictures while Twila finishes up?"

Twila laughed and shook her head at her mother's side eye that she shot at her father and his wife.

"Twila, what time is Josh coming?"

"He said him, and Jeremy will be here before the limo gets here so soon," Twila answered and looked at Adriana. Adriana sucked her teeth and posed for her mother's camera. Twila shook her head and giggled as Adriana mouthed Jeremy's name like she was going to be sick.

"Uh, speaking of your dates, here comes two handsome gentlemen now," Candice said while going to the front door and opening it wider to allow Josh and Jeremy in. Maddie sat up in her cage and began to growl.

"Not now Maddie!" Sharon called out.

"There she goes!" Adriana laughed as Maddie broke out into full blown barking.

"Hey, hey, it's okay, Maddie," Candice said soothingly as she walked over to Maddie's cage and sat down on the floor next to her. Maddie wagged her tail, loving the attention she was getting from someone other than Twila for a change. Sharon rolled her eyes and walked over to Twila.

"Hold your head down while I put the tiara on."

Twila shuddered, *I don't want to do this*, she thought quietly. The conversation she'd had with both Coach Davis and Ms. Hanks about the football team's secret popped into her mind, followed by the sharp needle she witnessed piercing into Josh's skin. Next, her mind wandered to the ultimate mind stealer, the death of James and the reason why he'd died.

"Dumplin'?"

"Yes," Twila answered cheerfully.

"Is everything ok? You haven't said two words to your guests."

"Hey Josh."

"Hey Jeremy."

Twila gave Josh a quick hug and sat down on the couch, finally ready to put the shoes of doom on her feet. "I hope I don't fall in these," she quipped while slipping them on.

"Was sup, Twila," Jeremy spoke.

"Hey Twila, you look pretty," Josh followed.

"Thanks."

"Okay now, let's get some pictures with you and your dates!"

Twila stood up and steadied herself, hoping and praying that she didn't embarrass herself and fall right in front of Josh.

"You got it," Josh asked and held out his hand.

"Yep, I'm good," Twila said with confidence, not wanting to hint that the shoes were a bit too much for her.

"Okay, Twila and Josh, y'all stand over there with Adriana and..."

"His name is Jeremy, ma."

"Yes, that's right, Jeremy. Okay, Josh and Jeremy, stand close to your dates so we can get a good picture. I'm going to have it blown up and put in a frame."

"Ma."

Twila looked at her father for help and on cue, he walked over to Twila's mom and stood beside her. "Why don't we go ahead and get it done so that the kids can be on their way?"

"Good Idea, Fred. That's what I'm doing."

Twila sensed the annoyance in her mother's tone so she slapped on her happy face and put her arm around Josh's waist.

"There you go! Get into it!"

Twila sighed internally at her mother's overly exaggerated enthusiasm.

Is your mother coming over Josh?"

"No sir, she took all her pictures and she said she would call Ms. Sharon later for details. She has an exam coming up and she needs to study while Ariel is at her friend's house."

"Oh okay, good."

"The limo is here," Candice smiled and took her position at the front door.

"Alright, y'all have a wonderful time and Twila, you are the best queen ever!"

Twila laughed and hugged her mother. "Thanks ma."

"You girls both look so pretty, and you boys are killin' it with the tux game."

"Ma!" Twila yelled, embarrassed that her mom was ready to talk in her "teen" lingo.

"What?"

"Have a nice time, Dumplin'; you look beautiful."

"Adriana, are you ok? Remember if there's triggers there, you know what to—"

"Ma, please," Adriana snapped and walked over to the door.

Twila rushed as fast as she could to Adriana's side. Not wanting her mother to embarrass her about her problems that she had last year. It was last year but her mother always found a way to bring it into this year.

Twila watched as Adriana's dad kissed her on the forehead and walked out, waving goodbye to the crowd. Going out behind him, Twila held on to the banister with one hand and to Josh's arm with the other. *Please don't fall...please don't fall,* she ranted while walking slowly to the limo. Another crowd gathered outside, anxious to see kids dressed up and ready to go. Twila smiled and waved at Kim and Paul, her neighbors from down the street, also on their way to the ball, as they got into their ride.

"Have fun!" Candice yelled.

"Thanks," the crowd said in unison as they slipped inside the limo.

"Finally!" Twila said as she adjusted herself in her seat.

"How are you doing Jeremy?" Twila said cheerfully, ready for get some conversation started between Adriana and her date.

"I'm good."

Twila looked at Adriana and motioned for her to join in. To no avail, Adriana looked out the window and sighed.

"Uh...okay," she quipped and grabbed one of the champagne glasses that lined the shelf in front of her.

"Oh word! They got champagne up in here," Jeremy perked up, smiling for the first time since they've been together. Twila looked over at Adriana, hoping that she wasn't uncomfortable.

"Are we allowed to drink any?" Jeremy asked.

"I don't know," Josh said. Let's ask."

"Aye, excuse me."

The driver rolled down the window. "Yeah?"

"Can we have any of these drinks back here?"

"Yeah, you sure can. Enjoy."

Twila looked over at Jeremy and then at Adriana. "Maybe we shouldn't. I don't drink and neither does Adriana."

Adriana smiled at Twila before turning her head and looking out the window.

"Get me that glass, Josh," Jeremy gleefully said while sitting up in his chair.

"You know Jeremy, you haven't said much of anything until now that you are about to do something stupid and have a drink," Twila said and shook her head.

Ignoring her, Jeremy reached over Twila and Josh and pulled out the bottle. "We 'bout to get lit up in here!" Jeremy grinned. Grabbing the biggest wine glass, his smile was quickly replaced with a frown once he saw the label. *Arbor Springs Sparkling Cider* spelled out in gold and white letters on the side of the bottle.

"Ha Ha!" Twila chuckled sarcastically and smiled at Adriana. *Lord knows she don't need any distractions*, she uttered internally.

Frowning, Jeremy put the drink back in its container and sat back in his seat. "Well," he said quietly. "So much for that."

Twila shook her head and looked at Josh and laid her head on his shoulder. "You good?" She mumbled.

"Yep, I'm good. What about you?"

Twila sighed, not able to fully remove the thoughts of Harriet High's football team and their secret. "I'm good, I guess."

"Dat's was sup."

The group remained silent until the car came to a stop. Looking out the window, Twila admired the dance committee's efforts to create the ultimate ball experience. Twila hissed at

Jeremy as he reached over to open the door. "Uh, the driver gets the door for us boy."

"My bad," Jeremy chuckled.

"Yeah, Twila, you know he don't know any better about stuff like that," Adriana joined in. The group laughed as the driver opened the door.

"Ladies first," he smiled.

Adriana hopped out first, Twila followed closely behind her. Standing and waiting for the guys, Twila looked around. Her eyes glistened at the sight of Kyle's memorial that displayed boldly on the school's lawn. Why do I always do that? It's been over a year and I still get misty eyed every time I focus on it. Fanning her eyes, hoping that the tons of make-up her mother plastered on her face wouldn't be ruined before she could even get into the school, she looked to her right and saw Josh finally walking towards her.

"Yo! Josh! Was sup!" A few of Josh's teammates ran over to him. Twila rolled her eyes as the team gave each other dap and laughed at basically nothing. Their dates walked ahead and entered into the school.

"Why did we even bother coming to this mess?" Adriana quipped and placed her arm around Twila, almost causing her to stumble.

"Girl! You know I can barely walk in these things," Twila snarled. "Now you gonna knock me down."

"My bad. I don't know why you didn't bring some other shoes just in case you don't make it. We don't need you falling on your ass like you did at the graduation."

"Ha, Ha, Ha," Twila said and rolled her eyes. Pulling her phone out of her purse, she hit her mom's number.

Can you bring me some flats please??????

Waiting for her mother's response, she looked around at more kids pulling up in limos and other luxury cars fixed up especially for the beloved dance.

I will get your dad to drop them off... he's getting ready to leave.

"Dang, daddy still over there. We've been gone for a minute now and he and Candice are still there. That's crazy."

K

"Maybe your mom is having a heart to heart with your stepmother."

Twila gave Adriana the meanest side eye she could give. "Yeah right. Hell didn't freeze over today."

"Y'all ready to go in?"

"Yeah, why y'all just standing here?" Jeremey walked up beside Adriana and put his arm around her.

"Take your hands off me!"

"What?! We goals now. Ain't that what y'all girls call it? That's what we are supposed to do, right?"

"Yo, you stupid, yo," Josh chuckled.

Twila laughed and turned her head.

"We are not like that. We are just here together at this dance and after this, we go back to not knowing each other." Adriana pushed

Jeremy's arm off her shoulder and walked to the other side of the walkway.

"Damn, it's like that?" Jeremy laughed.

"A'ight, so why y'all still standing out here?"

"Um, 'cause we are waiting for y'all," Adriana answered, not giving Twila a chance to respond to Josh.

Josh shook his head and slid his hand under Twila's, leading her into the school.

"Good evening…"

"Hi there… don't you look beautiful?"

Twila cringed at the voice who was throwing out compliments. Ms. Hanks stood in the middle of the hall, greeting every kid who crossed her path. "Ugh," she blurted and moved on the other side of Josh, as if that would keep her out of the principal's view.

"What's wrong?"

Twila glanced at Josh. "Nothing, I'm just ready to go. These heels are killing me."

"Okay, well let's go in and find a seat."

"Twila! You look beautiful! That's such a pretty shade of blue!"

Beginning to feel nauseous, Twila forced a smile. "Thanks," she said quickly and walked past as fast as she could. An array of colorful balloons sat in front the gym's door. A huge purple sign with the words:

An Enchanted Evening written in a deep orange displayed above the door. The sign was supposed to be inviting but in Twila's eyes, it was taunting and an invite for disaster. "Enchanting? Humph, yeah right," she hissed under her breath.

"Congratulations Twila!"

"Yeah congrats girl!"

"Thanks," Twila said shyly at two girls she barely knew; pretty much just seen them and didn't see them in her math class.

The door to the gym opened and Twila gasped at the sight of Coach Davis and Coach Snow standing side by side, smiling at the students. *Look at them. Standing there like they actually care about us.*

"How's it going girls?" Coach Snow spoke first.

"Hey," Adriana, Josh, and Jeremy all responded in unison. Twila remained quiet and moved over to where the tables were. Sitting down, she kicked off her shoes and massaged her left foot.

"This is nice," Adriana said while bobbing her head to an old school slow jam that was playing. "What's this called?"

"I Call Your Name" ... Switch," Josh answered and sat down next to Twila.

The group looked over at Josh, wondering how he knew about the jam.

Catching the question, he chuckled. "My mom listens to all the oldies."

Hmmm, Adriana smiled and continued to dance slowly in her seat. Looking around the gym, Twila began to massage her right foot as she took notice of the picture staring back at her. A picture of James in his uniform stood on the stage, right behind the king and queen's seats. Twila closed her eyes as thoughts of James lying in his casket came into focus, taking center stage in her mind. Choosing to focus on the sea of kids dancing out in the middle of the floor, Twila looked around at all the tuxedos and ball gowns, not paying much attention to the rhythm less bodies that were in them.

"Again, why are we even here?" She turned to Adriana and asked. "Nothing but lames here."

"Well, because you are the queen of tonight's ball! Get out there and dance with your king."

Twila looked at Josh, hoping that Adriana's comments about dancing with the king wouldn't sour his mood. Thankfully, it didn't. In fact, he seemed a bit dazed. "You alright Josh?"

"Yeah, I'm good. Was sup?"

"Nothing, you don't look—"

"Hey! How are you enjoying yourselves so far? I see you haven't gotten up to dance yet. Twila, shouldn't you be up there in your chair? You are the queen of this ball."

"We good," Adriana yelled, still vibing to the oldies.

"Okay."

Twila eyed Ms. Hanks as she stood in front of them, obviously thinking of something to conversate about. *Out of everybody here, she wants to chat with us. I'm guessing we are the only ones who knows what she and her hoodlum gangstas are up to.*

"Have you all had anything to drink?"

"We are ok Ms. Hanks," Twila said, not bothering to look her in the eye. *I am so ready to get out of here.* Sighing, Twila focused her attention on the groups of kids hanging around. A handful were dancing, while others were standing in small groups chatting and laughing.

"I'll be back, going to get something to drink. You want something?"

"I'm good Josh; thanks anyway."

"A'ight."

"Hold up, Josh, I'ma come with you."

I guess I should offer you something since we are—"

"Yeah, yeah, yeah, no thanks," Adriana cut Jeremy off before he could finish his sentence.

Twila glared at Adriana.

"Thanks for the offer," she said and rolled her eyes at Twila.

"There you go! I've been looking all over for you."

Twila smiled at the sound of the voice, not because she wanted to but because it was the polite thing to do. *I mean, he is the king and supposed to be my partner for tonight.*

"Todd, how are you?"

"I'm good, ready to get our dance in and my kiss. You ready to sit in our chairs?"

"Skurrr... hold up fool and slow your role! We ain't doing no kissing. I don't even know why they voted for you to be king."

"Whatchu mean?! 'Cause I got it like that. That's why!"

Twila waved her hand. "You don't..." leaning over to the side, she spotted Josh talking with Coach Davis. "No," she whispered as Josh said something to another one of his teammates and they walked away from the drink table, the coach following close behind them.

"If you would just get rid of that—"

Twila put her hand in Todd's face and stood up.

"What?" Adriana asked and followed Twila's eyes.

"Come on, Josh just went back and... just come on." Rushing around the table, she stumbled over her shoes. "Damn it!" Forcefully pushing the shoes off to the side, she grabbed Adriana's wrist and worked as fast as she could to get to the other side of the gym.

"What is it?!"

"Josh, he just went in the back with the—"

"Hey! There you are! It's time to salute this year's king and queen. Get on up there on the stage."

"Coach Sno… Coach Gardner with all due respect, I don't have time for this. I got stuff to do, so excuse me!"

"Aye! Twila, was sup?"

Twila felt like the room was spinning and she was losing full control of her senses. "Where did you go?!"

"Huh? Whatchu mean? I was standing over there at the drink—"

"No, you went with the coach and then you—"

"Twila, what are you talking about?"

"Over there," Twila pointed towards the table. Kids from all over began to crowd around Twila as if she was the main attraction at the zoo. The music quieted down and Twila heard the faint sound of kids mumbling, clearly about her.

"Twila, let's go home," Adriana said. "We don't have to stay. I will call your mom for you, come on."

"Josh," Twila started and looked him in the eye. "I saw you leave that table. Where did you go?"

"This chick is trippin'. I didn't go…"

"Josh!"

Twila watched in horror as Josh's eyes rolled in the back of his head right before he fell to the floor

"Oh God! Josh!"

A slew of people ran over to Josh, some tripping and falling over each other while others pulled out their phones, anxious to get some extra likes on their social media pages by posting Josh's incapacitated body.

"Somebody call an ambulance!" Someone in the crowd finally yelled.

"Hurry up!"

"Josh! Open your eyes! Come on Josh!" Twila begged and pleaded with Josh to wake up but to her dismay, he continued to lie there with no movement at all.

"Stand Back!" One of the custodians yelled as he dropped to his knees and began to feel over Josh's body. "Okay! He's alive, there's a pulse."

"Thank God!" Twila said in a hushed whisper. Pulling on Adriana's hand, Twila lifted herself up and stood. Looking around, she spotted Coach Davis and Coach Snow both running towards the back of the gym, in the direction of their offices.

"Dumplin'! Twila!"

Twila turned to the only voice that could offer her comfort. "Daddy!"

"Hey, hey, what's going on?"

"Daddy, it's a bunch of mess going on here." Twila looked around before she continued. "This school is crazy daddy!"

"Whoa! Slow down dumplin'. What's going on? What do you mean crazy?"

"Coming through! I need everybody to step back!"

Swarms of kids rushed out of the paramedics' path as they pulled out equipment and dropped to their knees beside Josh, ripping his jacket quickly. Twila gripped her father's arm while keeping her eyes fixed on Josh.

"What's wrong?! What happened?!"

"Something happened to Josh," Twila heard her father mumble to his wife.

"Oh no! Did someone call his mom?"

"Twila?"

"Um, no, I don't think... can you call her please?" Twila gave her stepmother her phone, jumping back startled as the paramedics lifted the stretcher. *He looks so pale*, Twila thought as she tightly held on to her father's arm.

"It's going to be ok Dumplin'."

Tears began to fall as she watched Josh being whisked away.

"Daddy, can you take me to the hospital?"

"Yes, let's go."

"Adriana, come on. I will take you home. Call your father and let him know."

"Okay Mr. Fred," Adriana responded before grabbing Twila and hugging her.

Look at them, standing around talking like they had nothing to do with Josh fainting... or with James dea... stopping mid-thought, Twila let go of Adriana and frowned at the stage taking notice of James' picture. Her stomach burned from the inside and bubbled its way throughout her body. In an instant, she lifted her gown up a few inches and made her way to the stage, glancing at the three people she held responsible for all the mess that was happening. Taking a quick study of James' picture, she grabbed the microphone and cleared her throat.

"Excuse me!"

Slow chatter continued throughout the room.

"Hey!" She yelled as loud as she could, immediately taking charge of the room. She saw her father walking over to the stage, so she knew that she had a quick minute to get the squabble that was going on her mind out of her mouth.

"They are telling lies and keeping secrets!" Twila looked over at the principal, Coach Davis, and Coach Snow before she continued, pointing at them. "They have been giving the football team steroids!" Gasps and surprised moans replaced the silence in the room.

"Dumplin', get down from there!"

"Daddy, those people have been giving kids steroids! That's why James is dead, and Josh is on his way to the hospital! They are the ones who caused it!"

"I don't know what she is—"

"It's true!"

The crowd twisted and turned to identify the voice who had cut Principal Hanks off. Todd walked up on stage next to Twila and took the microphone from her. "It's true... Coach Davis cut my boy Anthony from the team the other day because he told him he wasn't going to keep taking the meds."

"No, wait!"

"No, you wait!" Anthony yelled at Coach Davis and walked onto the stage, standing next to Twila. "You threw me off the team because I was tired of playing games with y'all."

Twila looked around the room, noticing looks of confusion from some of her classmates, amusement from others, and a determined look on her father's face while he was pressing buttons on his phone.

"I don't like needles and I don't like that stuff you and Coach Gardner were putting in my leg!"

"Coach Gardner? Who's that?" One of the kids whispered just enough for others to hear.

"You know...Coach Snow," her friend standing beside her answered.

The room suddenly focused their eyes on Coach Snow.

"I don't know what he is talking about."

"Yeah, you do," Todd replied. "All y'all know what he is talking about."

The crowd turned their eyes on Todd, anxiously waiting to hear what he had to add.

"All y'all are in on it. This wack crown that me and Twila got is not because y'all voted. Who even voted for king and queen?"

Twila looked in the direction of where her father was standing and noticed he was gone. Surveying the crowd, she found him whispering something to Candice.

"Whoever voted, y'all voted for nothing. Me and Twila was going to be king and queen anyway so we would keep our mouths shut. Ms. Hanks..." Todd stopped and looked over at the principal. "Ms. Hanks, she gave us king and queen so that we wouldn't tell anybody what we know."

More gasps from the crowd erupted, giving Todd a boost to continue. Josh popped into Twila's mind causing her to inhale deeply and exhale slowly.

"Ms. Hanks, Coach Davis, and Coach Gardner has been giving the football team steroids and laced brownies."

Twila whipped her head towards Todd so fast that she thought it was going to fall off. "Laced brownies?" She asked in a voice full of confusion.

"Yep, Coach Gardner is so good at making them. She adds just enough extra ingredients in them to keep the team calm enough so she can get the shots done."

Twila felt as if she was going to explode. *So, steroids and other drugs too*? Twila looked over at the trio she now referred to as the demon team.

"So now y'all know why James is dead...why Kyle was riding in the street the night..." Todd looked over at Twila and then out at Adriana before he finished his sentence. "Kyle was high the night of the accident; he'd just left from getting his injection and had one of Coach Gardner's brownies. He was out of his mind high when he rode his bike out in the rain and out in the middle of the street that night."

A single tear fell down Twila's cheek as she watched Adriana run out of the gym, with Candice right behind her. Twila breathed a sigh of relief when she saw her father's partner walk into the room along with four uniformed policemen.

One year later...

"Josh! Stop before you fall on your butt!" Twila laughed aloud as Josh attempted yet again to skate away from the wall and out into a sea of experienced skaters.

"Y'all stop being all scared and get out here!" Adriana called out as she whipped past, Todd trailing slowly behind her.

Twila laughed again and grabbed Josh's arm. "Come on, just hold onto me," she said and smiled.

"Okay, you better not let me fall."

Twila laughed again, "I gotcha!" Twila held onto Josh's arm for dear life, his legs no longer moved as good as they used to before his stay in the hospital after he was drugged for months. No longer on the football team, Twila took on the job as his personal rehab trainer away from his trainer at the hospital.

"Let's go back and sit down. My leg is starting to hurt."

"Okay," Twila replied while guiding him to the closest chair.

"You good?" Twila rubbed Josh's back while he caught his breath.

"Yeah, I'm good," he responded while rubbing his legs.

Twila chuckled at the sight of Todd working as hard as he could to keep up with Adriana. Adriana continued to leave him, showing off her skills with her skates and making small talk with one of the girls she met earlier.

"Looks like Adriana finally met somebody. Todd may as well give it up," Josh chuckled.

Twila nodded her head and leaned back in her seat, enjoying the happy and exciting view.

"Twila!"

"Ugh!" Twila huffed. "Yes?!"

"Don't forget to take Maddie out, I'm not doing again today!"

Twila shook her head. "Okay!" She called out while getting her diary out of her nightstand drawer. Throwing it on the bed, she walked over to her aquarium and sprinkled a few flakes into it. "Eat up guys," she smiled while walking back over to her bed and flopping down. Tiny scratches tapped on her door followed by a quick bark. *Just a few minutes, that's all I ask!* Getting up again, she quickly walked over to the door and opened it. Maddie slowly walked in and licked her foot. "Hey girl," she soothed. Twila watched Maddie as she sniffed around the bedroom, walked over to the window, and finally walked over to Twila's beanbag and laid down, huffing before she curled up in a small ball and closed her eyes. Smiling, Twila dropped down on her bed, picked up her pen, and opened her diary to a fresh page:

Dear Diary,

It has been a long year! I mean really long! I am so...

"Shoot!" Twila huffed as her pen began to fade. "Dang," she quipped. "And it's my favorite one too!" Reaching over to her nightstand, she pulled a pen out and quickly threw it back, opting to use a purple pen instead. Drawing a tester line on the top of her page, she went back to writing her entry:

I am so glad that Josh is back to normal. No more of him wilin' out on me now that he's fully clean and sober. I am so proud of him for all the work that he's been doing at his therapy sessions; getting stronger and stronger every single day. It's been hard being one of the ones blamed for putting Principal Hanks and her goons, Coach Davis and Coach Snow, in prison for drugging damn near half the school. They weren't just drugging the football team but the cheerleaders too! All for some competition that they clearly could've won by themselves... at least I think they could've... Twila chucked and shifted her weight before continuing.

It was no need to pump them full of steroids so they can do the perfect stance. Anyway... I can't believe I have to go to court and testify against my school! Daddy went in on those goons. Not just them, but the entire school! Who knew my daddy had that much power... well, him and his partner are detectives... I guess that's their job. Who knew that Harriet High would be all over the news... all on the map! (Mom is loving all the juicy news stories every night.) People were and still are talking about Harriet High, especially at my school...my private school. Ma and daddy snatched me out of Harriet High so fast after all that happened that I didn't even have time to say bye! Hmmm only if they knew all the crazy stuff that goes on in my new school... they would defiantly snatch me up out of there and make me stay right at home. I'll save that for another entry. Too much for this one.

Chuckling, she continued writing.

I'm happy that I can still chill wit' Adriana everyday even though she moved to her mom's house all away across town. (Thanks to her parents buying her a car and trusting her again to drive.) It's time for me to con my parents into getting me one. I am tired of riding around...

"Twila!"

Shaking her head, Twila put her head down and sighed. "Yes ma?!"

"It's getting late! I want you to walk Maddie before it gets too dark!"

Twila laughed as Maddie lifted her head, responding to her name being called. Slowly wagging her tail, she walked over to Twila and stared at her. "You and ma are working together," she chuckled.

Reaching behind her, she grabbed her pen and jotted *to be continued...* under her interrupted entry and closed her diary.

"Alright, let's go before ma has a fit." Maddie began wagging her tail faster, anxious to get out for her walk.

Yolanda's Note

ello Loves!

Twila was faced with so much in this story, starting with Josh and all his issues. Twila wanted to remain loyal and she did! But it was up to her as his friend, as his girlfriend, and as a fellow student to say something; to speak up for him! Josh's life was in a major crisis with the use of steroids and other drugs that put his life in danger. Thankfully, he was helped before it got to the point of no return; like James. James paid the ultimate price by abusing drugs and allowing his coach and others to give him the poison. Then there was the fact that she was in a fight with administrators at her school! For sure, that's a huge fight to fight but that's when it was time to reach out for some help.

If you find yourself in that type of situation, please reach out for help from someone who you can trust. Yes, school administrators are deemed people you should be able to trust but in Twila's story, they weren't the ones she could put on her list. Your parents, family, or other adult friends is a great place to start when you feel that you are in a situation over your head. There are people around that you can go to for help. You don't have to handle stuff all by yourself.

Although this book is fiction, there are a lot of cases where this type of situation is taking over. Remember, that you are strong and have the right to make decisions about your life. Never allow someone to dictate your life, other than your parents, and push you to a bad place. Drugs are no good and it certainly doesn't make situations better. It only makes situations worst. Use your strength within instead!

Love,

Yolanda

MEET THE AUTHOR!

Yolanda Randolph is the creator of the **#Her Intuition Movement**, a movement dedicated to empowering and motivating women to be at their best and to remind them of their worth. Yolanda is also a Credentialed Medical Coder, mother of three teenagers and the owner of Madisyn, her beloved Yorkshire terrier.

Yolanda is an avid reader and loves to write as well. She is dedicated to helping young women reach their highest potential through telling her stories. A survivor of domestic violence and many trials throughout her life, she has become persistent with encouraging others; in hopes that she is an inspiration.

Originally from Baltimore, Maryland, Yolanda now lives in Greenville, NC with her family.

Stay connected with Yolanda

- ❖ **Facebook-** *Yolanda Randolph Publications*
- ❖ **Instagram-** *Yolanda Randolph*
- ❖ **Twitter-** *YolandaRWrites*
- ❖ **Website-** www.yolandarandolph.com
- ❖ *Pink Roses* on Facebook and Instagram (A teen community)